EVERY SHOT I TAKE

Lessons Learned About Golf, Life, and a Father's Love

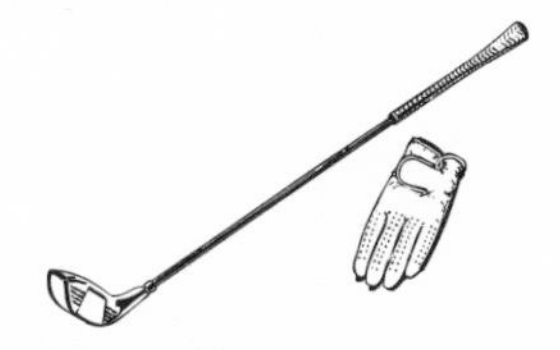

DAVIS LOVE III

Simon & Schuster

SIMON & SCHUSTER
Rockefeller Center
1230 Avenue of the Americas
New York, NY 10020

Designed by Deirdre C. Amthor

Manufactured in the United States of America

1 3 5 7 9 10 8 6 4 2

Library of Congress Cataloging-in-Publication Data is available.

ISBN 0-684-83400-6

For my mother:
Who gave my father all her faith,
and love, and friendship,
and somehow found
even more to give to me.

Contents

Acknowledgments

I've known all my life that a tournament golfer does not magically emerge, at age twenty-one, ready to shoot 66 and take on the world. There are, of necessity, people behind him, and people behind the people. In the past year, I've learned the same is true of a book.

My close friends and managers Vinny Giles and Vernon Spratley of Pros, Inc. have helped keep the idea of a book from my father's notes alive for many years. I thank them for their faith and guidance in all my endeavors.

My gratitude to Jeff Neuman of Simon & Schuster runs deep. Writing a memoir about my father was something I had been pondering a long time, but in the end it was Jeff's generous urging that made the book happen when it did, and his keen editorial instinct that gave the book the shape it has. Because Jeff edited the books Harvey Penick wrote with Bud Shrake, and because Mr. Penick was like a second father to my father, I knew Jeff would provide the necessary and best guidance this book could have.

Thanks, too, to Jeff's assistant, Frank Scatoni.

David Black, and all his colleagues at his literary agency,

helped make the business of being a rookie author a far less daunting task than being a rookie touring pro.

I also wish to thank Peter Paul Balestrieri of ASAP Sports, and Peter's colleagues Jerilyn Gargano, Marylin DiGeorgio, and Alice Dockery, for transcribing an enormous amount of material so quickly and so well.

My parents proved to me that there is nothing stronger than a family that works and plays together. The A. W. Jones family of The Sea Island Company has given all the Loves great support and inspiration over the last twenty years, and I am grateful to Bill Jones, Jr., for having my father come to Sea Island to teach, and changing our lives forever. His son Bill Jones III has become a dear friend and confidant, and his sage advice has served me well often, including on this book. I found his office at the Ocean Forest Golf Club to be a great inspiration, with its view of the course and the ocean breeze blowing in the window.

In my thirty-two years, I have only had three golf instructors, all of whom you will meet in this book. I thank Claude (Butch) Harmon, Jr., for his honesty, friendship, and teaching that made golf fun for me again after losing my father. And to Jack Lumpkin, who has put me on the road to greater things, I look forward to the journey together. I am certain that Butch and Jack have my father's thankful eye upon them. I have also learned countless lessons from many great teachers: Bob Toski, Jim Flick, Peter Kostis, Paul Runyan, Tom Ness, Scott Davenport, and many others. I thank them all for the kindness they showed my father and my family.

Robert Tyre Jones, Jr., once wrote, "You may take it from me that there are two kinds of golf, there is golf—and tournament golf. And they are not at all the same thing." In my tournament play no one has given more of himself than my brother Mark. To have a friend, a partner, and compatriot at my side under the strain of championship pressure makes the triumphs more rewarding and the disappointments easier to take. This book would not have been complete without his help.

To my lovely wife Robin, who I feel with me every minute of the day (even when she is outside the ropes), thank you for your love and patience. For Alexia and Davis IV, the true joys in my life, let this book tell you more of the grandfather you would have treasured.

Three years of college and eleven years on the PGA Tour do not make me an author. Author is a special title, as is golfing gentleman. Michael Bamberger is a fine example of both. I once said that I would only do this book with Michael, thinking that a wistful fantasy. I thank Jeff Neuman for putting us together, and Michael for doing an inspiring job bringing this story into its final form. Michael, you told me, "Have a son, plant a tree, and write a book." I am honored to have worked with you and finished the list.

Davis Love III
Sea Island, Georgia
January 22, 1997

CHAPTER 1

My Dad's the Pro

I had driven the ball into the trees. This was not uncommon for me. My father used to say, "The woods are full of long hitters," so Dad always knew where to find me. Someday, he promised, he would teach me to be a straight hitter, too. But at this moment we were looking for my ball among the tall pines of coastal Georgia, on a golf course owned by the Cloister Hotel at Sea Island, where my father was a teacher of golf—and some other things, too. I was a guinea pig for a lot of his ideas, his best pupil in some ways, his worst in others.

We found the ball and I surveyed the shot and surveyed my father. He was never one to state the obvious; his eyes, even through his glasses, said all I needed to know: I was dead. The only things between my ball, sitting on a bed of pine needles, and the hole were trees and trouble. I took out a 3-iron, made a big, violent pass at the ball, and hit it cleanly and well. The ball rose quickly, passing one tree on the left, whizzing by another on the right, over a third tree, soaring into the daylight until it reached its apex. There, my ball made a soft righthand turn before landing 20 feet from the flagstick, which stood at attention 220 yards from where my father stood in awe.

"Of all the millions of people who play this game," my father said to me, "the two most exciting are Seve Ballesteros and you."

I was a kid, a teenager. Seve Ballesteros was one of the best players in the world, maybe the best, a winner of the British Open and the Masters. He was one of my heroes.

Analyzed rationally, my father's praise was absurd; there was no sensible way to discuss Seve and me in the same sentence. But my father did, and in so doing he made me the golfer, and the person, I am today. Seve is no longer a hero to me; he's a colleague, a friend, a competitor. He's another guy I'm trying to beat. My late father, for whom I am named, is still my hero. He always was; he always will be.

I wish every golfer could have the kind of golfing education I had. I wish every child could have the kind of father I had. If someone could grant me those wishes, the world would be a better place, and scoring averages would be a lot lower, too. I miss him. Writing this book has made me miss him more. Today, people who follow professional golf in the United States know my name, and that's nice, but to me it was always my father who was the famous one. Everywhere we went, people knew him, people admired him, people respected him, and I knew at a young age that I wanted those same things for myself. As a little kid I'd say to people, "My dad's the pro!" And they would nod and murmur, "Yes, son, we know that." The way he introduced me to golf is the way I plan to introduce my two children to the game. The way he taught me is the way I plan to teach them. The way he raised me is the way I hope to raise them.

One of the things I remember best about him is his hands. Dad had the most amazing hands. He never wore sunscreen or golf gloves and he was outside all day long, all year long, and he always had a golf club in his hand, so his hands were really dark and really tough. I can remember as a little kid, walking hand-in-hand with my father, how hard his skin was, like the skin of a lizard. I used to love to poke at his calluses. You couldn't make a dent in them; they were like a piece of leather left in the rain and then baked in the sun. Now my children—my wife Robin and I have a daughter, Alexia, who was born in 1988, and a boy, Davis IV, who was born five years later—do the same thing with my calluses—they poke pins right in them. They think that's sport.

My father wore a rather peculiar expression on his face most of the time. It was like a serious smile, as if he was enjoying what he was doing, but what he was doing was serious. You seldom saw his whole face unobstructed. It seemed as though from the moment he woke up in the morning until he went to bed he wore his glasses and a white or light blue bucket hat with the brim down, to cover his mostly bald head. (Of course, he took the hat off inside and when he talked to ladies. There was a lot of Old South in him.) But even with the glasses and the hat, when you looked at his face you noticed right away that his eyes were alive. They were always moving. There was always light in them.

Dad was kind of fidgety. The only jewelry he ever wore was a plain gold wedding ring, and he was always fiddling with it. When he gave lessons, he was always jangling the change and the keys in his pocket. That sound drives me berserk to this day. I'm not temperamental on the golf course about crowd noise, but when we're playing on a cold day and the old men in the gallery have their hands in their pockets, jingling, jingling, jingling, it makes me crazy.

(Now that I think about it as an adult, I think the reason my father was so fidgety was that he was probably addicted to nicotine, even though he wouldn't even admit to being a smoker. The fact is, he smoked a fair bit, he just never *bought* cigarettes. If he was giving a lesson and he saw something green in somebody's pocket—Kools, Salems, whatever—he'd go right for it, bum a cigarette from a complete stranger. Then he'd run off to the snack bar or behind a tree and sneak a quick smoke. I think he honestly thought my brother, Mark, and I didn't know that he smoked—as if we couldn't see the billows of smoke coming from behind a tree, as if we didn't see Dad popping out from behind the tree when he was done, as if we couldn't put two and two together. It bothered Mom that Dad smoked, and rightly so. He wasn't a drinker and never used profanity but he was addicted to cigarettes. Cigarettes and ice cream—those were his vices. He snuck his cigarettes because he didn't want us to see them. Looking back, it makes me realize that he wasn't perfect. But as best he could, he tried to present himself as a model.)

My father read, all the time. He loved to read. Golf books. Books about philosophy. Self-help books. Books about religion. Detective novels. He loved to read Elmore Leonard and Ed McBain and Stephen King. I think you pick up the habit of reading from your parents. I love to read now, too. Once at a tournament I was talking to Frank Hannigan, the TV golf commentator, and I said, "That reminds me of that Hunter S. Thompson story about . . ." Hannigan interrupted me and said, "You read Hunter S. Thompson?" I said, "Sure." And he said, "Well, you and I are the only two out here who do." My father felt reading could take you to places you wouldn't otherwise know existed.

Because he loved to read, he loved to write. When he died in a plane crash in 1988 at age 53, he left behind closets and cabinets filled with loose pages and legal pads containing his notes about the golf swing. I go back to these notes often. Most of the ideas expressed in this book can be traced, in some form, to something written somewhere on one of my father's legal pads. He used the long ones and he preferred yellow, but he'd use white, too. He'd also use envelopes and hotel stationery and the back of shopping lists, if that's all that was available.

Whenever my father had an idea, he wrote it down. He was interested in many things, from the lyrics of country music to the afterlife of the soul, but it was the golf swing that motivated him to put pen to paper. He felt that if he didn't write an idea down he might lose it when the next one popped into his brain. He believed in the written word. Over the years, he wrote many instruction articles for *Golf Digest*; he was a longtime member of the magazine's teaching staff.

Dipping into my father's notes, I find hundreds of pages where he recorded my every shot in a round in a shorthand that wouldn't be intelligible to anyone but me. I see outlines for instructional articles. I see inspirational letters for me filled with little sayings. I see lesson plans.

One page looks like this:

KEEP THIS—READ OFTEN—
USE WHAT YOU NEED MOST

1. Let your attitude determine your golf game. Don't let your golf game determine your attitude. [That was probably his favorite saying about the *playing* of golf.]
2. Our emotions get in the way of doing for ourselves what we would like to do for others.
3. Don't be afraid to be a kid—have *fun*.
4. Don't let self-esteem get mixed up in golf score; golf is different from life.
5. Don't run away from yourself. Wherever you go, there you are.
6. There is nothing you can do to lose our love.

On another sheet he had written only this:

Knowledge is power. The more we know, the better. Study language. Direct relationship between vocabulary, income and success. Learn new words.

His lesson plans for me might look cryptic to somebody else, but not to me:

WATSON "POP" STROKE

1. Don't let eyes follow backswing.
2. Swing putter back shorter than through.
3. Listen for ball to drop.
4. Clear and firm—decisive stroke.
5. Always have a positive thought.

In longhand, those five lines mean that to imitate Tom Watson's putting stroke, the key to which is the "pop" he gives the ball at impact, you have to do five main things: While making a backswing, you must keep your eyes on the ball, not the putterhead. Also, the backswing must be shorter in length than the follow-through. After you make impact with the ball, don't look at the hole, look at the spot where the ball was, and then just listen for the ball to drop. Once you decide on the line of the putt and how hard to hit it, don't be tentative, know what you want to do with the stroke and do it. Always believe you can hole the putt; don't attempt a putt you don't believe you can make.

An outline for an instructional article about the difference between "hitting" a golf ball and "swinging" a golf club included these notes:

1. Ben Hogan was the best *hitter* I ever saw, but nobody can *swing* like Ben Crenshaw.

2. Swing like you were being paid by the hour, not the job.
3. Some golfers might be able to "hit" the ball from a very forward position, but their "swing" wants the ball back a few inches.

The legal pads, as in the examples above, were filled with sayings from his mentor, Harvey Penick, and from other teachers. My father had many original ideas, but he also believed that the teaching of golf should be done with colleagues, that ideas should be shared, and that good ideas should be repeated and incorporated, regardless of where they came from. He felt the teaching of the golf swing—but not the golf swing itself—was a complicated task because students had such widely varying needs. Therefore, he felt the discovery of the best approaches to teaching required a team of scientists, a group effort.

But there were other times, as his notebooks reveal, when he was all on his own. When he made the biggest professional decision of his life, to leave the security of the head professional job at the Atlanta Country Club to become a fulltime golf teacher, he weighed the pluses and minuses—on his legal pads, of course.

CONS	PROS
More uncertainty	More freedom
Lean years/good years	Potentially more pay
Leave friends	Love teaching
More time on road	When home, more time with boys

He made the move, and I think the last item in the second column had a lot to do with his final decision.

Golf was a father-and-son thing for him, too, sort of. He grew up in El Dorado, Arkansas, and his dad, who traveled a lot on business, was a weekend golfer. My father would caddie for his father when he was home, and Dad became smitten with the game. He became good at it, too; he played golf at the University of Texas under Harvey Penick. After serving in the army in Korea, he became a club pro. His first head professional job was at the Charlotte Country Club in Charlotte, North Carolina, which is where he met my mother, Penta—she was working as a secretary for the pastor of the First Baptist Church in Charlotte at the time. I was born in Charlotte, in 1964, on April 13, the day after the last round of the Masters in which my father shared the lead after the first round. (He shot 69, as did Arnold Palmer, Bob Goalby, Kel Nagle, and Gary Player. He finished in a tie for 34th, no doubt worried about Mom back at home.) In 1965 he took a job as the head pro at a new club, the Atlanta Country Club. Mark was born in Atlanta the next year. In 1978, he got out a legal pad, made his lists of pros and cons, and moved the family to St. Simons so he could teach golf at The Cloister and for the *Golf Digest* Instruction Schools, which were held all over the country. One of the reasons he wrote out so many lists was that he always wanted to build a consensus in the family before making a decision. I try to do that in my house today and it drives Robin crazy. She'll say, "Would you stop all your talking and just make up your mind!"

My first memories of golf go back to Atlanta. Our house was on the course of the Atlanta Country Club. From our backyard Dad could hit pitching wedges to the second green and drivers to the third green. The ball just seemed like it was going miles, and I remember the terrific whistling sound it made as it left the clubface and went off, soaring. He worked at golf and played golf all the time. Mondays were his only day off. He'd put me on the cart and I'd watch him practice while I goofed around with clubs and balls. Work and play, I think those words meant the same thing to me when I was a real little kid. Dad would say, "I'm gonna go work on my putting, wanna come?" I always wanted to come, because Dad's "work" was fun.

He was an only child, and I don't think he had that much fun growing up. His father was an imposing man, very serious. When we went to visit our grandfather as kids we had to put towels down on the back seat of his big black Chrysler so we wouldn't mess it up. In his own way, I think my father spent his life revolting against his father's dourness.

I think that's why he devoted his life to golf: Golf is fun. Of course, it's also incredibly exasperating, but it's fun. Whenever I'd go out for a round, particularly an important competitive round, he'd say, "Have fun." Those weren't empty words. He meant them as much as anything he ever said.

Years later, whenever I would say, "I've got to work on my long putting," or some such thing, he'd say, "Don't think of it as work. Think of it as play." That's why he loved his profession so much. He didn't regard it as work. He enjoyed giving golf lessons.

When I was a teenager, I used to go with him, when I could, to his *Golf Digest* Schools. A lot of the guys he taught with—Paul Runyan, Bob Toski, Peter Kostis, Jack Lumpkin, Jim Flick—are considered today to be the leading teachers in the game. But teaching golf day after day can make a man crazy; the golf swing can be very elusive to some would-be golfers, and that can take its toll on an instructor. Dad's colleagues all marveled at his disposition.

When they taught chipping at the *Golf Digest* Schools, they had a little phrase for their pupils: *Minimum air time, maximum ground time*. It meant that when chipping you should get your ball on the ground as quickly as possible, that it's better to chip with a 7-iron than a pitching wedge. One day Peter Kostis was explaining this approach to chipping to a pupil, and when he was done the student, a grown man, asked, "Peter, do you really believe it's important to get the ball on the ground as quickly as possible when chipping?" Kostis went nuts, and I could understand why. It *was* frustrating. Kostis started kicking buckets of balls. He was foaming at the mouth and screaming, "What have I just been saying here for the past 15 minutes?" My job was to pick up the students' practice balls with one of those shag-bag plungers, and I very sheepishly went off to collect the balls Peter had just sent flying all over the place. My father came over very quickly, settled Peter down, and told the student, "You ask if we believe in minimum air time, maximum ground time. It's a good question. We certainly do. It's one of our maxims." Dad was a peacemaker.

Episodes like that were critical to my golfing development. I was not a golfing child prodigy. Before I was nine or ten, I was mostly just fooling around with the game. The only thing my father worried about was that my golf not interfere with somebody else's. Aside from that, he let me do whatever I wanted to do, which included a cross-handed grip for one stretch of time and a baseball grip for another. I'd play a few holes from the ladies' tees when the course wasn't crowded. There was very little talk about score, although if I made a bogey, say, on any given hole I was showered with praise. I would say, though, that from the very beginning, my dad—and my mom, with whom I played often—told me about the rules. *You tee up behind the markers, Trip*, which is what they called me. *You don't touch the sand with your club, Trip. You keep hitting the ball until it goes in the hole, Trip*. They didn't care if it took five shots or a dozen. But they could see that I was enjoying it. I also enjoyed hockey, reading, watching TV, going to baseball games, goofing around. I didn't pursue the game with some crazy monomaniacal vengeance. *That*, I think, my father would have worried about, at least at that age.

Then, in the summer after I turned 10 in 1974, I went with Dad to the PGA Championship. That was an eye-opener. My father played in the tournament, and I was mesmerized by the atmosphere, by the idea that there were gallery ropes and only the *players*, like my father, were allowed to go inside them. The players hung out in the locker room, telling stories while changing into shiny, expensive shoes. All the stars of the game were there, and my father knew them and they knew him. Gary Player. Lee Trevino. Nicklaus and Palmer. Newspapermen wanted to talk to these men, kids wanted their autographs, and my father would chat with them like they were the guy down the street who was thinking of buying a new used car. I thought to myself, "Man, this is the life."

After that, I started playing more. I'd play 18 holes on some days, and on other days just a few. Every so often, I'd go to the practice tee and hit a few balls, or putt a little on the practice putting green, but I had no formal instruction from Dad. My father never really started me in golf; he just made clubs and balls available to me and brought me out to the golf course whenever I felt like it. If I asked him a question, he'd answer it, in as few words as possible. I realize now that what he wanted me, and Mark, to do was enjoy the game for the game's sake and see for ourselves what works and what doesn't work. When I was 10 I shot mostly in the 90s. When I was 11 I shot mostly in the 80s. When I was 12 I could break 80. I was just playing. I had dreams of the tour, but I never thought about the effort and time necessary to get there.

Then, when I was 13, we moved to St. Simons, and things changed. That's when I became serious about golf. On St. Simons, we again lived right near a golf course, but things were different now. My father wasn't a businessman anymore. He wasn't selling merchandise out of the shop. All he was doing was trying to figure out the swing and figure out the best way to teach it. Having moved to a new place, I didn't have the distraction of a whole gang of friends pulling me to do this and do that. My father's fascination became my fascination. One day, I told my father I didn't want to play hockey anymore, and that I wasn't interested in playing football and soccer, like Mark was. I told him that all I really wanted to do was get good at golf. And my father asked me, and this has become part of our family lore because it was a pivotal conversation, "How hard are you willing to practice?"

I said, "I'll do whatever you think is necessary."

And Dad said, "I'll help you reach your goals. But you've got to listen to me." I did and he never had to say those words again. He wanted to make sure I knew and understood what I was getting myself into.

After that, my golf became much more regimented. Dad would say, "Let's go to the practice tee and see what you're doing with your fairway woods." Dad and I would stand on the tee of a par-3 and he would say, "If the wind is blowing left to right, and the flagstick is on the extreme right, where are you going to start the ball?" Dad would say, "Let's hit five balls out of the bunker from the same lie with the clubface in five different positions."

But one thing Dad always stressed, above everything, was that golf was supposed to be fun. He said it often and he meant it. He had me do a lot of drills, like hitting with just my left hand, or just my right hand, because he knew the drills were a challenge and that I loved challenges, but chiefly because they were good for my golf, and they were *fun*.

He would have me hit balls in all sorts of strange ways: Standing on my left foot. Standing on my right. Sitting in a chair. Trying to hit a driver just 100 yards, but straight. Trying to hit a 5-iron 300 yards without caring where it went. Half-shots—my father was big on half-shots. He reasoned, quite accurately, that if you can't hit a hip-to-hip 7-iron straight, you won't be able to hit a full one straight. Conversely, if you *can* hit a half-shot with a 7-iron straight, you're halfway to hitting a full 7-iron straight. When I got out on tour, I sometimes forgot how all these drills served me so well, but when I'm at home, they come back to me. Trying odd things is a great way to stumble onto something basic about the game that may stay with you the rest of your golfing life. When we practiced our putting we made a game of it. The same was true for chipping and bunker shots and everything else. We played for ice cream. When I was 13, 14, 15, my father didn't give me 45-minute lessons starting with, "Today, son, we focus on the pivot." It was more like a steady stream of little suggestions about this and that, always said in the fewest words possible. I never knew I was getting lessons.

Probably the most important single lesson I ever got from Dad came shortly before we moved to St. Simons. It taught me what golf meant to my father, and how golf is meant to be played. It probably paved the way for everything that my dad and I did together thereafter.

I was 12 going on 13, and the family was together having dinner at home, as we always did. My father asked me how I had played that day after school.

"Uh, I shot 36 today," I said.

My father looked at me carefully and said, "Thirty-six? Even par? That's quite a score. I don't think you've ever shot even par for nine holes before."

I had shot 36 for eight holes. Our house was near the eighth green of the Atlanta Country Club course and I didn't play the ninth because I was too lazy; I didn't want to walk all the way back from the ninth green to the house for dinner. I had quit after eight holes and 36 strokes.

"Isn't that right, Davis?"

I didn't say anything.

The next day, he started telling the guys in the pro shop, in front of me, about how I had played nine holes in even par for the first time in my life. I felt sick. I never lied about a score again in my life. I never lied to my father again. I didn't know then what I'm sure of now: *Of course* Dad knew that I hadn't shot 36 for nine holes. If I had, I would have sprinted from the ninth green all the way home to tell him the news, and he knew it. I think another father might have said, "Are you telling me the truth about that score?" There's nothing wrong with that. My father's approach, though, was different. His lesson took quickly, and will stay with me forever.

This memoir of a teaching pro would be incomplete without my father's teachings, his lessons and stories, his fables and theories. Many of the golfing tips in these pages are from my father's notes, items that have been tucked away in filing cabinets for years. Others are from a Southerner's oral tradition, stories told and retold on practice tees and putting greens and in grill rooms, stories that I'm glad to have down now on paper. All these little items have two things in common: They've been helpful to me, and I think they'll be helpful to you.

A TIP FOR MY MOTHER

Some golf teachers are afraid of giving "tips." Some teachers think of tips as Band-Aids for more serious swing maladies. Not my father; he thought of a swing tip as a manageable, insightful way into a golfer's swing. He was a great believer in tips and he knew you had to try out a lot of tips on a player in order to find one that would really sink in. Like with my mother, for instance. People naturally assume that I was the pupil my father was proudest of, but the truth is my mother was his best student ever. He took her from a raw beginner, with no particular bent for sports, to a formidable player. Even now, approaching 70, she breaks 80 pretty much every time she tees it up, and she's particularly strong on difficult courses on blowy days. I asked her once what was the single best golf tip she had ever received from Dad. She didn't hesitate to answer: "When the club is at the top of your backswing, your left thumb must be underneath the shaft, supporting the shaft." That is absolutely correct. A good golf swing cannot be made with the thumb anywhere else. Whenever my mother's swing goes awry, she goes back to that basic thought and gets herself back on track.

THE FEEL OF THE SWING

My father always believed that the ultimate beauty of golf is that it's a sport that can be enjoyed by all people, not just by "natural" athletes. Even on the tour, there are many players who are not natural athletes, who can't hit a baseball, or make a jump shot, or run very fast. One advantage that the natural athlete has is his ability to feel a golf swing instinctively, because natural athletes seem to have a heightened sense of rhythm. The rest of us, myself included, have to learn to feel the swing.

One of my father's best methods for doing this was a drill in which he would hold a club vertically in front of him with his left hand. Then he would throw a ball sidearm with his right hand underneath his left hand. Try it. That motion you just made with your right hand? The way your feet just moved? The way your hips just rotated? It's called the *golf swing*, and the basics of it are in just about all of us. When he would tell beginners that, their mouths would drop open.

BALL POSITION

Every golfer has one ideal ball position in his or her stance. The old adage was that you pretty much played the ball off the left heel, maybe moved it back a few inches as you approached the pitching wedge. My father felt that one size did not fit all in that regard. He would have his pupils take a swing without a ball, and make sure they took a divot. The beginning of the divot indicated where the ball should be positioned.

A BASEBALL SWING

Most Americans, men and women, are introduced to baseball or softball before they take up golf. A common lament among teaching pros is, "Uh-oh, this guy has a baseball swing." My father always felt a baseball swing could be applied very usefully to the golf swing, particularly when trying to teach how to get a golfer's weight through the ball. He'd have a golfer address the ball in the normal fashion. Next he'd have them bring their left foot back to the right foot. Then he'd have them step into the swing, as if they were hitting a baseball, making certain that the left foot returned to its original position. The correct leg motion is critical to a balanced, powerful swing—and good leg action can happen naturally, if you allow it to. My father knew that baseball gave you some natural movements a pro could build on.

When I first started playing golf, like most kids, I used a baseball grip, and I used it for years until my father showed me the Vardon, or overlapping, grip I use today. Since the grip is such a critical component in building a proper swing, I've often wondered why he didn't get me away from the baseball grip earlier. I got my answer when my son Dru was just two years old. He's an exceptionally athletic little guy who could hit a plastic baseball with a plastic bat by his second birthday, and he did it with the prettiest little swing you ever saw. But when it came to golf, he was always chopping at the ball; he'd hold the club up over his head and chop down on top of it, as if he were chopping firewood. One day on the practice tee at Sea Island, Louise Suggs, the legendary golfer who was one of the pioneers of the Ladies Professional Golf Association, was watching Dru do his chopping bit. I asked Louise, who knew my father, for help. She turned to Dru and said, "I know you love baseball. Can you make a baseball swing with your golf club?" Dru gave her a big nod and made a baseball swing with his club. "Good. Now can you put the club behind the ball and give me another baseball swing?" Dru did just that. "Beautiful!" Before long, Dru was flying the ball 15 to 20 yards. By his third birthday he was hitting it 40 yards in the air. There's not much difference between a golf swing and a baseball swing, except that a baseball swing is parallel to the ground and the golf swing is not. After Louise said that, I remembered how useful my father said it was to have a beginning student who played baseball or softball as a kid. He'd say, "Did you play baseball as a kid?" If the answer was yes, he'd say, "Wonderful."

OTHER PEOPLE'S MISTAKES

If you spent enough time with my father—I spent a *lot* of time with my father, and now my only wish is that I had spent more—

sooner or later you would hear him say something about the role of just about every part of the body in the golf swing. This is what he said about the right leg: "Use the right leg as a brace; turn your swing around it. The right leg barely moves; it always keeps its flex." One of the things that made him a great teacher was that you could always say to him, "Why?" Sometimes he had a very philosophical answer for you, sometimes he had a numbingly mechanical answer, and every so often he'd just say, "Over the years, I've found this works best. Every time I've seen a straight right knee on the top of the swing, I've seen bad shots." Through my father, I was able to learn from other people's mistakes.

ONE SET OF HOLES

Sometimes golfers may sound a little neurotic to nongolfers, but sometimes we have to be, in order to make ourselves understood. For instance, my father felt it was fine—important, actually—for the left foot to come up in the backswing. But he also thought it was critical for the left foot to return to its original position on the downswing. To express this thought to me, he'd say, "You know the holes your cleats make in the ground when you address the ball? When you begin the downswing, and your left foot returns to the ground, I want the cleats in the same holes they were in originally."

ALIGNMENT

My father found it amusing that professional golfers spent a lot more time on swing basics than the average amateur. He knew that that shouldn't be the case. And to him, one of the most basic of the basics is alignment. If you're not aimed properly, hitting a straight shot is all but impossible. In fact, a straight shot from improper alignment is, actually, an off-line shot. Before you make any swing, there's a final step you should take to make sure your shoulders and hips and legs and feet are all aligned properly: If you're aligned properly, you should be able to just rotate your head, move your chin from six o'clock to nine o'clock, and have your target come immediately into view. If you have to twist and cock your head to find your target, there's something wrong with your alignment.

OBSTACLES

One of Dad's favorite phrases was, "Faced with an obstacle, do not ignore it, overcome it!" Those ten words have many implications beyond golf, but on the course they are incredibly useful too. There were times in my golf career, particularly when I was starting out, that I didn't give enough weight to the obstacle I had to overcome. I thought if there was a tree I had to bend a ball around, I could will the tree away and, with it, my problems. After hitting many trees resulting in many bogeys, I realized the truth to my father's words: You cannot ignore an obstacle, you must figure a way around it.

This is true in how you approach learning different aspects of the game, too. If you can't play downhill greenside bunker shots—and not many players can—then that's an obstacle you must overcome, one that can't be ignored. Go to an able teaching professional and say, "Teach me to play downhill greenside bunker shots." That's a lot better than praying that you're never going to face that shot—because sooner or later, you will.

Obstacles can be pretty subtle sometimes. You might have a

caddie who is reading greens for you when you don't want him to. After a while, all you're thinking about is your precocious caddie and not your own golf game. Don't ignore it, overcome it. Say to the caddie, "I appreciate your effort, but when I'm unsure of the read on a putt, I'll ask. Thanks."

A QUIET HEAD

Some people will do anything to keep their head down during the golf swing. Sometimes you see a guy who sticks his chin into his chest and keeps it there for the entire swing. Not a great look! When nongolfers would meet my father, they might say, as a way of making conversation, "Gotta keep your head down, right?" Golf's greatest myth! A golfer's head may move during the swing; Ben Crenshaw and Curtis Strange, two of the best golfers of my time, move their heads a lot. The head may come up at impact; Annika Sorenstam, the women's U.S. Open champion, doesn't even see the ball when her clubhead makes impact with it. The head should not be frozen, my father would say. But it should be "quiet."

My dad's favorite drill for teaching a "quiet" head was a drill he called Right Foot, Left Toe. My goodness, it seems like a goodly portion of my youth was spent on RF-LT, as we called it in the house. He'd have me address the ball with my feet together. Then he'd have me drop my left foot back and have my left toe point into the ground and my left heel up in the air. Then he'd have me make little half-swings in that position and ask me to be aware of what my head was doing. You can't move your head too much with that foot stance, or you'll wind up on the ground.

ADVICE FOR TEACHING PROS

Dad was a meticulous man, determined to always improve himself. That's why he was always writing himself notes, and I'm just so glad that he and my mother saved them all, or most of them, over the years. Going through his notes, I found one he had typed for his own use during his early days in the business, when he was head professional at the Charlotte Country Club. I'd like to share it with you because I think it gives an insight into how he analyzed situations, and I also think it offers some sound advice for teachers and students alike:

- Talk to your member on the way to the practice tee. Find out what he shoots, what his problems are, and what he wants to get out of golf. Not every player wants to be the best golfer in the world. Many members do not have the time or inclination to completely revamp their swing. They do not want to go through the drudgery of mastering major changes in their swing, so don't be too anxious to condemn or criticize any and every moment in their swing that deviates from the "normal" or the "correct."
- Any move in your member's swing that repeats can be used to his advantage. No matter how wrong it looks, think long and hard before tampering with any part of the swing that consistently repeats. You can build around this motion and produce an effective swing because repetition is the key to success in this game, whether or not it conforms to the "standard" swing.
- Stay away from major changes, unless it is in your junior program.
- Teaching with criticism is the easy way out, but not the most successful. Be a creative teacher! Put all your en-

ergy and enthusiasm into every lesson you give and you will find that you will reap benefits not only in satisfied customers and increased lesson business, but also increased shop sales as well.

SPRAY PAINT

Dad never went anywhere without a can of spray paint, and it's not because he was a graffiti artist. He was forever drawing lines on the grass of whatever practice tee he was standing on. The line would show the shape of the backswing and follow-through. On the backswing, the line would go straight back from the ball for a few feet, then curve gently in. On the follow-through it would go straight to the target. He'd have his pupils swing along these painted lines in practice. With enough practice, the lines would "appear" in your mind's eye on the golf course. That's the best way to get to know the proper swing path.

Once I asked him, "Dad, what would've happened if you hadn't discovered spray paint?" He said, "I would've had to pay a lot of money in college tuitions." In other words, Dad felt that Mark and I became the players we did—good enough as seniors in high school to win golf scholarships for college—because we had down the principle of a good path and a good plane. Everything flows from that. But you don't really need a can of paint to perfect your plane and path; you can lay down clubs, grip end to clubhead, or you can use tape or string. Regardless, when you're learning about plane and path, get something tangible to help show you the way.

NOT JUST ANOTHER STUDENT

Jack Nicklaus, Jr, a.k.a. Jackie, the oldest son of Jack and Barbara Nicklaus, was on the golf team with me at the University of North Carolina. Jackie and I have very similar physiques—tall and skinny and flexible—but Jackie's swing was modeled after a man much shorter, thicker and stronger than he is. (Any guesses who?) Jackie would sometimes seek my father's swing advice and Dad would answer his questions, but in a very quiet voice. The son of Jack Nicklaus is *not* just another student. What my father told Jackie was that he, like me, should try to keep his left heel on the ground as much as possible, because that helps create stability for a tall, skinny, flexible golfer. Dad had another observation, though, that he would never have told Jackie: There was no way Jackie could or should model his swing on his father's, just as I could not model my swing on *my* father's swing. In both cases, the physical differences from one generation to the next were too considerable. Over the years, I observed that Jackie's swing started to look less like his father's and more like, say, Al Geiberger's, a tall, skinny, flexible man. Jackie developed into a good player; in fact, in 1985 he won the North & South Amateur, the same event I won in 1984. As I watch my son take to the game, I'll always bear in mind what my father said about Jack and Jackie Nicklaus.

ADVICE FROM A LEGEND

Because of my father's job, I had a privileged youth in many ways. As a teenager, I got to play once with Sam Snead. Sam didn't say much, if anything, about my swing, or even my length, but he did say one thing I'll never forget: After watching me play an iron shot on a par-3 without the benefit of a tee, Snead said to me, somewhat derisively, "Son, I've never seen a player good enough not to use a peg when the rules give it to him. Not yet, anyway." Before that, I always thought I was cool in teeing up the ball on a little tuft of grass on par-3s. After that, I've never *not* used a "peg."

FEEL THE ARMS

To understand the golf swing, my father always said, you had to *feel* the role of the arms in the swing. To teach that, he had to find a way to momentarily take everything out of the swing *except* the arms. To do that, he had his pupils hit balls with their feet together. That forces you to hit the ball with just your arms. As a teenager, I hit so many balls with my feet together that when I finally separated them, I had the sensation of, "OK, what do I do with the rest of my body?" But at least I understood that controlling the arms is how you control the direction of the ball.

A NATURAL REPELLENT

Where I grew up playing, in coastal Georgia, there are a lot of gnats. We'd often hit balls with gnats gnawing away at our legs. It was awful. My father's way of dealing with the pests was to take some lit cigars, the cheapest and most malodorous he could find, and prop them up around us. The air may have smelled like a fraternity poker game after that, but at least we weren't getting eaten alive.

THE LEFT ARM

How important is the left arm in the swing? Consider these words from my father's notes, words that are probably in the notes of every instructor the game has ever had: "As much as possible, make the club an extension of the left arm."

OUR FAVORITE DRILL

My father said it was critical to make practice fun, and the most fun we had was practicing the height of our pitch shots. Dad would park a golf cart near the edge of a practice green and have me hit balls over the roof, under the roof, over the back rack, past the front wheel, anything we could think of. It's very important to learn to hit pitches different heights because the height of a pitch shot will determine how much the shot rolls. A 25-yard pitch shot over a greenside bunker to a tight flagstick is a much different shot than a 70-yard pitch shot over flat, firm fairway to a flagstick 25 yards back from the front edge of the green. I think I know where my father got this idea: When Mark and I were kids, we used to hit pitch shots into garbage cans in the backyard. My father stole this drill from his sons!

CHAPTER 2

"Do What Tom Kite Does"

I wasn't a great golfer through most of my high school years. I didn't do anything in the national junior tournaments. I was long and wild off the tee and my putting game was poor. For my freshman and sophomore years, I attended a private school on St. Simons, the Frederica Academy. As a freshman I was shooting in the high and mid-70s. As a sophomore I was shooting in the mid- and low-70s. The school was terrific academically but there wasn't a lot of competition for me in golf, so for my junior year—after a long series of conversations with my mother, trying to persuade her that we weren't placing a higher emphasis on golf than academics—my father and I decided that I should transfer to the nearest public high school, the Glynn Academy, over a causeway and 10 miles away in the old port city of Brunswick, Georgia. In retrospect I would have to say Mom was correct: for good or for bad, we were putting golf ahead of academics. My father thought highly of the Glynn Academy for one basic reason: He admired the golf coach, Herman Hudson, immensely.

At the time, the only thing that bothered me about the move was the Georgia rule requiring a student who transferred to sit out for a whole year before he could play sports. So all my junior year I practiced with the Glynn Academy and went to the matches, but I couldn't play in them. There's nothing to get the juices of a teenage golfer flowing more than being in that frustrating position.

In the fall of my senior year, when I was applying to colleges, there was nothing really to suggest I would someday turn into a Ryder Cup player. Fortunately for me, a high-school record in golf doesn't often reveal what kind of golfer you might mature into. For every Jack Nicklaus and Johnny Miller and Tiger Woods, all of whom were phenomenal teenage golfers, there are people like Paul Azinger, who couldn't break 80 in high school, or Calvin Peete or Larry Nelson, who didn't even play as teenagers. I was a decent schoolboy golfer, certainly not spectacular, but the college coaches could see that I was well trained by my father and by coach Hudson, and that I had a good work ethic and would probably improve. Several colleges recruited me.

And then, toward the end of my senior year, after I had already settled on the University of North Carolina at Chapel Hill, I started to make some really good scores. My last eight competitive rounds in high school were all in the 60s. I won the 1981 state junior title in Georgia. My game was improving not because of any specific thing my father and I were doing on the practice tee, but because of the truth of what my father said on our rides over the causeway to the mainland: "Competition will make you better." I was also improving because the Glynn Academy played its home matches at the Brunswick Country Club, an old Donald Ross course with hard fairways and small greens where you had to really golf your ball with discipline in order to make good scores.

My father and I decided on Chapel Hill for six main reasons, all of them listed at various times on my father's legal pads: First, Chapel Hill had good academics and that mattered, because there was no reason to think I'd make a living as a touring pro then. Second, the school was offering a scholarship, and although my father could have afforded to send me wherever I wanted to go, it would have been tight; we were perfectly comfortable, but we were by no means rich. Third, the school had a wonderful golf course. Fourth, the campus was 90 minutes by car from the North Carolina golfing mecca of Pinehurst, where there were *many* wonderful courses. Fifth, Chapel Hill was close enough to St. Simons that I could get home easily, but far enough away so that I could have some independence from my family for the first time in my life. Sixth, North Carolina had a great basketball team, and I loved ACC basketball. I had a job as an usher at basketball games. I gave Michael Jordan his first set of clubs.

My father used to say that you learn golf all the time, but you don't learn it all at once. During my freshman year at Chapel Hill, I was playing with a great deal of confidence, because of the successes I had had at the end of my senior year. Things I had been hearing and trying for years were suddenly totally clear to me. My game was making substantial gains. I learned to control the speed of my swing, particularly with the driver, and I started hitting a lot more fairways, which is a sure first step to making more pars and birdies, and fewer bogeys. In the spring of 1983, as a freshman, I was named an All-America golfer—an honor I received again as a sophomore and a junior. Over those three years, I won eight college tournaments. I won the ACC Championship twice. In the summer of 1984, before the start of my junior year, I won a prestigious national event, the North & South Amateur.

Then, as a junior in the spring of 1985, came a turning point. I was playing in an ACC tournament and I had a chance to win, but I made a bogey on the second-to-last hole and I missed a five-foot birdie putt on the final hole to finish a couple of shots out of first. I was really disappointed, and as I came off the 18th green the

Chapel Hill golf coach came up to me and said something like, "You would have had a good tournament if you didn't give up coming in."

I said, "What?"

"You quit on me," he said.

My father had taught me the value of keeping my composure. He taught me to respect authority figures. But he also taught me to stand my ground. In this instance, I went ballistic. One thing I *always* did was to try my best on every shot. That was just basic to the way we were taught the game: play by the rules, including the rules of etiquette, and try your best on every shot.

I stared my coach down. Veins were popping out of my neck. I said something like, "Are you *serious*? I give *everything* I have on *every* shot. I just puked my brains out trying to hole out my approach shot to the 18th green. I have *never* given up on a golf course in my life and if you don't know that after three years, I don't know what you do know."

My mother, who had been following me, came up to me and said, "What was *that* all about?" I really didn't know, although I did know there must have been a lot of pent-up animosity between the two of us. He may have resented that every time he told me something about the game I tried the idea out on my father before reaching a conclusion on its value. I think I resented that I was basically putting his golf team on the map and not getting credit for it. Everything spilled out in that one moment, in the wrong way, on both our sides. I had never spoken to an adult like that before. Of course, I had never been accused of giving up before, either. I knew right then I would never come back and play my senior year. The scale is different, but it was almost as if Michael Jordan, after scoring 28 points, had missed two overtime free throws resulting in a one-point North Carolina loss and Dean

Smith went up to him and said, "Nice foul-shooting, Mike, you just blew the game for us."

I knew my career as an amateur golfer was over. I could feel it inside me. It was instinctive; I knew in my heart it was time to turn pro. I had just turned 21. The odd thing was that I was making the biggest decision of my life—the first major decision of my adult life—and I wasn't consulting with my father. We weren't making lists on one of his legal pads. I was winging it. It was probably the first time I realized that my father and I, for all our similarities and for all my dependence on him, were very different men.

When I explained the situation to him, he could not have been more understanding. He was upset that I was leaving on bad terms and that I wasn't going to get my degree. (The truth is that I was losing interest in the classroom, because I was so focused on golf. I regret now that I didn't take my schoolwork more seriously, and I hope and plan to someday return to Chapel Hill to earn a bachelor's degree in English.) But no matter what my father's feelings were at the time, he understood my frustration and respected my decision. His attitude was to never look back, always ahead. He said, "Let's make a list of the things you need to do to prepare yourself for your professional career." Classic Dad.

Here's what he put on the list:

OFF THE COURSE
Be more organized/Manage your time better
Be more aware of your diet/Exercise more
Don't chase easy money/The tour is your livelihood

ON THE COURSE
Hit more fairways/Hit more 1-irons
Learn how to use yardage book/Get a good caddie
Know how far each club goes/Limit club experiments

I retained my amateur status through the end of the summer of 1985. I played in the Walker Cup, held that year at Pine Valley, in New Jersey, maybe the most interesting, demanding, and beguiling course I've ever played. It was at Pine Valley that my length got national attention in the golfing press for the first time. The fifth hole there is an uphill par-3, about 225 yards from the back of the tee. Some of the Walker Cuppers could not reach the green with their best 3-wood. I was playing it comfortably with a 3-iron. On the U.S. team with me were three U.S. Amateur winners, Jay Sigel, Scott Verplank, and Sam Randolph. Colin Montgomerie was on the Great Britain and Ireland team. He was already an impressive player and an intense competitor. We won, narrowly. Probably the biggest winner was the course and the golfing public, who got a glimpse of Pine Valley's greatness. The demands of the competition and the course served as an important training ground for me.

Several weeks later, I turned pro. That meant passing up an opportunity to play in the Masters; in those days, all U.S. Walker Cup players were invited to play in the following Masters tournament, provided they were still amateurs. It was a significant sacrifice, but I had no choice. It was time for me to play golf for my livelihood.

To earn a place on the PGA Tour you have to prove you have enough golf skill to deserve the spot. The most common way to earn a tour card is to go through a 162-hole golfing hell known as the tour qualifying school. Initially, there were 825 players competing for 50 tour cards. After a series of regional 72-hole tournaments, that number was reduced to 162 players, who gathered at the Grenelefe Golf & Tennis Resort, near Orlando, Florida. After another 72 holes, the field was reduced to 105 players. Then there was one more day of competition to see who would finish among the top 50, and in what order. The player who finishes first can pretty much play in any tour event he wants for a year; for the player who finishes 50th, the opportunity to get into events is much more sporadic. The qualifying school is an incredible grind because it's so long and exhausting and you have to play defensively; lose your head for a moment and you're playing the mini-tours for a year.

Dad walked with me every hole the whole way through, and Mark, who was just starting his sophomore year at Chapel Hill, caddied for me. The courses at Grenelefe were long and relatively open; they suited me. I opened with a 66, blew up to a 74 in the second round, and played unspectacular, steady golf after that. I finished sixth and earned $3,325, my first check. I was a pro. I was going to be on tour. Dad didn't give me much of a chance to celebrate. He said, "I think you're good enough to finish among the top 75 on the money list." He got out his legal pad and started up a list. "These are the things you need to do if you're going to win on tour."

To Win

1. Drive straight for a week.
2. Play within yourself.

He made another list. "These are the things you need to do to win consistently."

To Win Consistently

1. Drive straight regularly.
2. Play *your* game week in and week out.
3. Enjoy being in the hunt.

And a third list. "These are the things you need to do to become a dominant player."

To Dominate

1. Know you can win even when your game is off.
2. Have immense belief in yourself.
3. Have a happy, satisfying family life.
4. Improve your short game *a lot*.

I was maybe on the verge of resenting that he couldn't let me enjoy the moment. And then he said, "I know you can become a dominant player. You have a fantastic talent. I'll always be there to help, to give you as much help as you want."

After turning pro, one of the first things my father and I did was to settle on an agent. I signed on with Pros, Inc., in Richmond, Virginia, a company run by Vernon Spratley and Vinny Giles. We both knew Vinny, who won the U.S. Amateur in its final year of medal play, 1972. I didn't want a big, impersonal agency; Pros, Inc., was courtly and gentlemanly, and they were good businessmen, but they weren't sharks. Their philosophy is to always, as we say in the South, leave something at the table, in the interest of creating long-term good will. I've been with them from the beginning and I can't imagine going elsewhere.

As a rookie, I decided to play Ping clubs, Titleist balls and glove, Footjoy shoes, and Aureus clothes. I also represented the Cloister Hotel at Sea Island (and always will, I'm sure). Later, I played Tommy Armour irons, the 845 model, and I played well with them, but in 1994 Armour wanted me to switch to a new model they were promoting, a so-called oversized club, and I wasn't interested in doing that; I wanted to get away from a perimeter-weighted cast club. I started playing Titleist irons in 1996; the company devised a set of irons exactly to my specifications, perimeter-weighted *forged* irons that I designed, and no company had done that for me before. For a while, I was Titleist's star player. Then they signed a real star, Tiger Woods. That's how it goes in business.

Though my father wasn't much interested in business, he certainly understood the importance of money. One of the reasons he wanted to leave the Atlanta Country Club, where he was beloved, was that the club's management was trying to reduce his percentage of the pro shop revenue. But when I turned pro, Dad gave me the soundest business advice I've ever received: Concentrate on improving your golf, and everything else will take care of itself. He was dubious about the value of my competing in long-drive contests, or playing in corporate outings or giving exhibitions for pay, because he thought they could all take a toll on my play.

Dad gave me one other excellent piece of advice before I headed for California at the start of 1986 for my first West Coast swing: "Do what Tom Kite does." My father admired Tom Kite a great deal, probably because Kite and his game reminded my father a lot of himself and his own game. Tom was a Texan, born and raised, and he played his college golf for Harvey Penick at the University of Texas. Dad and Tom shared a mentor. Tom was also a Pros, Inc. client.

Dad called Tom before I got out on tour. Their conversation went something like this:

Dad: "Tom, I'm wondering if you'd do me the kindness of showing Davis around a little bit when he gets on tour. Do you think maybe you could play a practice round with him, show him the ropes a little bit?"

Tom Kite: "I'll play with him, but he better not be coming out here to goof off. If he is, we're not doing anything together, I don't care whose son he is."

My father got off the phone and said, "OK, he's willing to play a practice round with you, show you around a little bit. You go up to him and say, 'Mr. Kite, do you think we could play a practice round together?' And then you do exactly what he does."

Harvey Penick gave Tom some of the sagest advice any player could ever receive: Go to dinner with good putters. By that, Harvey meant hang out with good players, do the things that good players do, and your own game will improve. When I got on tour, I was trying to apply that advice to myself. I saw Tom at my first tournament and said, "Mr. Kite, may I play a practice round with you?" I was 21, and he was one of the most accomplished players in the game.

Then I became his shadow. When he practiced long putting, I practiced long putting. When he practiced pitch shots over bunkers, I did the same. When he and his caddie, Mike Carrick, paced off distances, double-checking the yardages in the yardage book, I did the same. I learned how to learn a golf course from Tom. Whatever hotel Tom stayed at, I stayed at. We've had a nice relationship ever since and it's become symbiotic; there's no other player on tour who knows my swing as well as Tom, and I think I know almost as much about Tom's swing as Tom does. We help each other.

The summer after my junior year I started dating Robin Bankston, and we got more serious over the course of my rookie year on tour. We were good friends in high school, but she would never have considered me boyfriend material then. She was the most beautiful girl in our class, and I was this dorky, string-bean golfer. But I guess through our college years her tastes changed, or I changed, or *something* happened. Just when I was heading into this great unknown, the pro golf tour, she finally started taking me seriously. She even came to the tour school; my dad, Mark, and I shared one room, and Robin had another.

When I decided to go on tour my parents asked me if I wanted them to sponsor me for the first year, or if I should go to various

Sea Island golfers we knew and see if they were interested in bankrolling my first year. I thought it made more sense to keep our business in the family. At the same time, I was thinking very seriously about asking Robin to marry me. My parents were not eager for me to marry as a tour rookie; they felt Robin and I were too young. They felt the adjustment to tour life and to married life would be too much in the first year or two I was on tour. They liked Robin a great deal, but they felt I should slow down. They said, "We can afford to sponsor you for a year, pay for your hotel and your travel and your caddie and your entrance fees. But we can't afford to send you and Robin out on tour. We think you should hold off on marriage for now, get your feet wet, put some money in the bank, then think about a wedding date."

I knew there was logic in what they were telling me, maybe even wisdom, but my heart was telling me something else. I went to my first professional tournament, the Bahamas Golf Classic at the Paradise Island Golf and Country Club, in the first week of January 1986. Robin was with me. I finished third and earned $24,000. In one week, I had made enough money that I didn't need to borrow a penny from my parents to get started on tour. I felt I had enough financial security to ask Robin to marry me. We got married at the end of my rookie season, on November 22, 1986. Mark was groomsman. My father was my best man.

There could not be two more different people than Robin and my father. Robin loved to stay out late, to entertain people, and to be entertained. She was definitely *not* into making lists and plans. And my father adored her. For one thing, he realized that I loved her and if he didn't he was going to lose me. But he also thought she was good for me, that I was happy and relaxed with her. At this point, pretty much everything with my father and me revolved around improving my golf, and he knew that alone was not enough to satisfy a 22-year-old. He took Robin under his wing before my mother did; Mom resisted Robin a little at first, because they were so different—over the years, they've become good friends—but my father didn't. He taught her how tournament golf works, how to figure out the cut, what a player goes through when he's in contention; he was starting from scratch because she had no background in the game at all. He even gave her a car. Money was tight for us, and my father had an old Grand Prix that he didn't need, so he just signed it over to her. He was so supportive. Early in our marriage, when Robin got pregnant with Lexie, she went to my father—well, I'll let Robin tell that story later.

Dad urged me to be really candid with Robin about what tour life was going to be like. I did just that, right from the beginning, and that's been one of the foundations of our marriage. I told her, "What I'm trying to do, to be successful in professional sports, is one of the most demanding things a person can try to do. I'm going to be away a lot and we'll be traveling a lot and it'll be a grind, but I have a goal to be the best player in the world and it's a very difficult journey and I'm going to need your help and support." At the time, she had no idea what I was talking about. She turned to my father for an explanation.

Dad said, "Everything Davis is saying is true, but he's forgetting one thing: You're going to have a lot of fun, too." And he was correct.

Despite my dour predictions, Robin and I had a wonderful time. We stayed in Holiday Inns and rented cheap cars and didn't order dessert if we felt our entrees were too expensive—and we enjoyed ourselves thoroughly. I had traveled quite a bit as a kid, going to junior golf tournaments, so the idea of living out of a suitcase was familiar to me, but Robin had never had the chance to travel and everything was new and exciting to her. She was meeting people she never expected to meet—actors, athletes, singers, from Roger Clemens the pitcher, to Bob Hope the legend. She was going places she never expected to go: Hawaii, the California desert, even Hattiesburg, Mississippi. She was seeing things she never expected to see: the Pacific Coast Highway, Niagara Falls, Las Vegas. It was a blast.

In my working life, I was nervous only occasionally. My locker in the clubhouse, assigned alphabetically, would often be near Bruce Lietzke's, and I'd watch him tie his shoes with some awe, because he was already a legend. He was a guy who didn't play very often, and was usually in contention whenever he did play. Sometimes on the practice tee, if I found myself hitting balls next to, say, Jack Nicklaus or Tom Watson, I'd be a little nervous when I realized those guys were *watching* me a little bit, seeing how far I hit it, trying to figure out why.

On the course, particularly on Thursdays and Fridays, I felt comfortable; I played my game. On the weekends, particularly if I was on the leaderboard with a bunch of household names, I'd get excited, but in a good way. As a matter of fact, I feel the exact same emotions today, and if I didn't I'd be worried. The biggest surprise to me was who played well and who did not. I began to realize that there wasn't much of a relationship between what a guy's swing looked like and where his name was in Monday's newspaper, or what a guy was doing on the practice tee and how he scored.

Dad spent a lot of time on tour that first year. I know that some people in their early twenties don't like having their parents around, but I was just the opposite. It was wonderful being on the practice tee at tour events with my father. A lot of the other pros would come by to see what we were doing, or to say hello to my father, or to see if he were available for a lesson.

For us, things weren't too much different from what we had been doing all along. He had me hit drivers off the ground. He had me hit 7-irons with my left hand only. He had me do his Left Foot, Right Toe drill, and his Right Toe, Left Foot drill. I was never embarrassed to do these drills in front of my fellow touring pros; we were all out there trying to do the same thing, trying to get better.

It must have been about halfway through my rookie season that I said to my father, "Dad, if I'm going to make it out here I'm going to have to improve my short game *a lot*." Of course, all I was doing was mouthing back to Dad the words he had suggested to me before I made my first paycheck. My father never mentioned that; all he did was get out a legal pad. "Let's make a list," he said.

To Improve Short Game

1. Lessons from Jack Lumpkin on chipping, bunker play, putting.
2. More time with Dr. Bob Rotella, learn more about mental approaches to the short game.
3. Watch tapes of Ben Crenshaw at the 1984 Masters.

I did all three things on Dad's list, and I was on my way.

THE KEY TO DISTANCE

The question I hear more than any other is, "How do you hit the ball so far?" The implied question is, "What can I do to hit the ball farther?" With the emergence, first of John Daly, and now of Tiger Woods, I don't hear those questions as much as I once did, but I hear them a lot and I understand the logic behind it. Hitting the ball as far as you can is important, as long as you're hitting it straight. It's easier to hit a ball on a green with a 3-iron than a 3-wood, and it's easier to stiff a shot with a 9-iron than a 5-iron. I find it a lot easier to break par on courses where I can get home in two shots on the par-5s than on the courses where I cannot. You should *want* to hit the ball as far as you can; don't be ashamed of that.

To some degree, every golfer stands in awe of the golfer who can hit it farther than they can. In the end, of course, you have to make the best with what you have, and that's why Corey Pavin is one of the greatest players in the game, even though there are literally hundreds of pros across the world who can blow it by him. My father was a good tournament golfer who was more interested in teaching than touring, but he was not a long driver. He probably hit the ball even shorter than Corey. When I started getting long off the tee, I could probably outdrive him by 80 or 90 yards, and I know he was a little awed by that. I mean, he made me the golfer I am, but he couldn't teach me length.

Once, I was playing in Florida in the tour qualifying tournament, the Q School. On a 440-yard hole, a dogleg, I cut off the angle and left myself just a little pitch shot into the hole. My father paced off the drive. It was 334 yards. Later he asked me, "How did you do it? You looked like you were swinging so easily, yet the ball went so far." I was really surprised. My father, who had spent most of his life around golf, sounded just like one of my pro-am partners who had been playing the game for a year. I answered, "Dad, all I was trying to do was hit the ball on the fairway. To do that, all I was trying to do was hit the ball dead in the middle of the clubface." That's really all you can do.

Extreme length is sort of like extreme running speed, I believe. It comes from within; it can't be taught. My friend Brad Faxon is stronger than I am, he can run faster, he can jump higher, he has more endurance on a bicycle, he probably has better eye–hand coordination than me. But I can drive the ball 30 yards past him consistently. (My wish is that I could putt like him.) What can be taught is the ability to hit a ball as far as you can, and I suppose both Brad and I do that. When I tell amateurs that to hit the ball far, what they need to do is hit the ball straight, they're disappointed, but it's the best answer I know. The long shots come off the center of the clubface, the same place where the straight shots come from. With the driver—with all my clubs, really—I try to hit the ball with about 80 percent of my overall power. The reason is that at 80 percent, I've discovered, I have a much better chance of hitting the center of the clubface with the ball, and the center of the fairway some moments later.

DO'S AND DON'TS FOR A HUSBAND AND WIFE

One of my father's oldest friends, in every sense of the word, was Paul Runyan, a prominent tour player in the years before World War II, the winner of the PGA Championship in 1934 and 1938, and the winner of the tour's money title in 1934—with $6,767. When I got on tour, Paul wrote out for Robin and me, by hand on stationery from the Holiday Inn in Augusta, Georgia, a list of suggestions for us under the heading "Do's and Don'ts for a Husband and Wife Team on the Tour."

For Robin

1. Be sure not to surprise Davis with any errands you need him to do before he goes to play, as this may upset his practice schedule with serious consequences for the rest of the day.
2. Help Davis at day's end to get his mind off golf for the rest of the evening.

3. Suggest and prepare a proper diet and rest schedule for Davis as to give him the best possible mind and body for play.
4. Do anything you can to bolster Davis's confidence in himself.

For Davis

5. The best way to avoid bogeys is to play a course intelligently *and* aggressively.
6. Put in a good day's work every day, taking into consideration how much work you can do without becoming exhausted. You've done too much when you can't recover with a good meal and a good night of sleep.
7. Never forget what made you: your golfing skill. Don't take on too many other activities that may interfere with your pursuit of golfing excellence.

For Robin and Davis

8. If driving, try to relieve each other on an hourly basis.
9. Avoid any argument or unpleasantness before play. Settle any misunderstandings in the evening. If you can't, declare a moratorium before bedtime.
10. Be sure you young people work as a team. Anticipate and recognize each other's needs.

STAND PROUD

When I'm practicing at tournaments, I'll sometimes hear people in the gallery say, "Hey, take a look at Davis Love. He looks like he's got a stick up his . . . spine." And it's true. My mother's father was a proud, tall farmer from North Carolina with very erect posture, and from the time I could walk I've walked just like him and my father was glad of it. He felt that when addressing a ball, a spine must be straight, and that it cannot lean to the right or to the left. Whenever he saw a golfer hunched over a ball on the practice tee, he had the urge to say, "Stand proud!"

THE HITCHHIKE DRILL

My father often gave his swing thoughts names. One he called The Hitchhike Drill, and there's a good illustration of it in the instruction book he wrote with Bob Toski called *How to Feel a Real Golf Swing.* The purpose of the Hitchhike Drill is to teach a golfer the spinning motion that is central to a good golf swing. All you do is place your right hand behind your back and your left thumb on your right shoulder. Now, in a spinning motion, move your left thumb to your left shoulder. That's the golf swing in miniature, and you don't need a ball or club to try it. You can do it anywhere. Sometimes I find myself doing the Hitchhike Drill in airports and hotel lobbies, or in the truck while I'm waiting for my daughter Lexie to get out of school.

DRIVERS OFF THE GROUND

To help me learn control of the pace of my driver swing, Dad had me hit balls off the ground. The clubhead must be moving perfectly level to the ground and perfectly square to the ball to get the ball airborne. Dad was only able to see me play in one Masters, in 1988, but he loved watching the crowd watch me hit drivers off the ground on the practice tee into the net that keeps the practice balls off Washington Avenue. The net is 300 yards away. At first, I was hitting drivers over the net. Then my dad tired of watching me show off, so he told me to move the ball to the ground. The crowd was oohing and ahhing and saying things like, "And the kid ain't even got a tee!" Dad loved it. On our way off the practice tee, a man asked my father, "What happened to Davis's driver? Did he break it? First he was hitting 'em over the net; at the end they were only reaching the net." The man didn't realize that I was doing my father's Driver Off the Ground Drill.

A PLEASURABLE DRILL

My father had one very relaxing and pleasurable drill for improving our putting: He'd have us watch highlight tapes of the 1984 Masters, the year Ben Crenshaw won at Augusta for the first time. You'll never see more holed putts, or a more syrupy stroke.

GRIP PRESSURE

My father's protégé at Sea Island, Jimmy Hodges, was one of my best friends. My father and Jimmy died together in their plane crash. One way I hope they will live on is by future generations of golfers using the ideas that Jimmy and my dad had about the game. Their greatest joy would be to know that future golfers are getting as much enjoyment out of the game as they possibly can.

I think of Jimmy often, for many reasons, but I think of him with particular connection to one problem all golfers have from time to time, particularly when they're anxious: gripping the club too tightly. The myth is that by gripping the club hard you'll hit the ball further. To hit the ball far and straight, you have to *feel* the clubhead, and you can only feel the clubhead when the grip is light. To illustrate this point, Jimmy would tell his pupils to grip the club really hard and waggle the club; the club feels like air and you can't control it at all. Then gradually lessen the grip strength until you're barely holding on to it. Now the clubhead feels like a sack of potatoes. Somewhere in the middle there is perfect grip pressure. As a general rule, lighter is better. But there are limits; I've experimented with extremely light grip pressure and I came to the conclusion that you couldn't control the club if you didn't hold on with some level of firmness. When I asked my father about this he said, "A grip should be like a good, firm handshake. Not so hard as to hurt somebody's fingers, but not so light that it's like shaking hands with a dead fish, either." Sam Snead's old chestnut on the subject was, "Hold the club like you've got a little birdie in your hands." The idea was that you don't want to choke a bird in your hands, but you don't want the bird flying away on you, either. My father taught occasionally with Sam at the *Golf Digest* Instruction Schools, and he enjoyed Sam's rural analogy—these days, how many people have ever actually held a bird in their hands?—but he didn't think it was precise enough. He wanted no tension in any part of the grip or stance or swing; tension prevents motion, he'd say, tension robs distance. But having said that, he wanted some real firmness with the last three fingers of the left hand on the grip. He felt you needed firmness there in order to control the swing with the left arm. People look with amazement at photographs of such extremely strong golfers as Fred Couples, John Daly, or Laura Davies hitting a ball with their right hand off the club. They amaze me too, but when I look at those pictures I also point out the firmness with which these strong golfers grip the club with the last three fingers of their left hand. Sam Snead was nice and firm with those three fingers, and you'll never see a better left arm through the ball than Sam Snead when he was at the top of his game.

WHERE CONFIDENCE COMES FROM

When I first got on tour, I quickly realized that some players played with a great deal of confidence while others looked nervous and tentative. Then I realized that the players who looked confident were the players who were playing well. I wondered, "Where, exactly, does the confidence come from?" And then I remembered my father's answer: "Confidence is born of proper practice." If you practice well, if you can do the things on the practice tee that will be demanded of you on the golf course, then you can play with confidence. And if you can play with confidence, you can play well. A friend of mine saw Joe Paterno, the legendary Penn State football coach, at Disneyland the day before the 1995 Rose Bowl. His players were goofing off, hanging out with Mickey Mouse, riding rollercoasters, eating pink food, having a good time. Coach Paterno was miserable. Somebody asked him, "Say, Joe, why the long face?" And he answered, "We had a lousy practice this morning. And you can't expect to play well if you don't practice well." So true.

KEEP ON TRACK

There was a wonderful image that my father used to explain how to aim: Imagine a set of train tracks that run from your ball to the target. The ball is on the outside track. Your feet are on the inside track. Your knees and hips and shoulders are aligned to the inside track. On a straight shot, you aim your clubface at the target, and your body to the left of the target, right down the inside line of the track.

A LITTLE AT A TIME

My friend Brad Faxon was once talking to a writer friend of his, trying to help him understand the nuances of what it means to be a touring pro, what it means to be trying always to improve on your craft. Brad said, "Can you imagine trying to learn everything about writing all at once? Same with the golf swing." My dad often said the same thing, but in a different way. He'd say, "Develop one part of your game, and then move on. Improve one thing and move on. Golf is a circle. Keep moving to the next station. Sooner or later, you'll come back to where you were, then that part will need attention. Don't try to perfect any one part of the game. That's a sure road to burnout. Just improve, and move on." Harvey Penick used to say, "Golf is a game you learn best a little at a time."

THE POWER OF THE PENCIL

One reason I chose Vinny Giles to be my agent was that my father had so much respect for him, both for the quality of his golf and for the way he carries himself. Vinny had the kind of golf game where people were always asking him why he didn't turn pro. In his prime, he had the ability to shoot in the mid-60s on any course on any day. Good scratch golfers will sometimes ask Vinny to evaluate their games, to see if they have what it takes to get on tour. Vinny's standard response is, "The game gets a lot harder when there's a pencil in your hand." In other words, for a good player to shoot level par on his home course with his friends in good weather from the members tee—that's nice, but that's not tournament golf. In tournament golf, you have a pencil in your hand; you're keeping track of your playing partner's score and he's keeping track of yours. Everything you do on the course will be reflected with your marker's pencil strokes. There is no place to hide. The pencil records all.

KEEP IT SIMPLE

My father had a weakness for ice cream, and he used ice cream in some of his golf analogies. For instance, he'd say of different ways to play a shot, "Pralines and cream is nice for a change, but for my daily ice cream I'm very happy with vanilla." (He probably heard that from Harvey Penick, who used the same metaphor.) He meant, don't make a shot fancier than it needs to be. I've known good amateur golfers who, facing a regular 5-iron shot to a flagstick that's in the middle of a green, say, "OK, I'm going to hit a high fade here that's going to carry the bunker by three yards and bounce to the right and leave me just below the hole with a 10-foot uphill putt." This from a player who hits a natural low draw! I feel like saying, "Hey, you're 190 yards away; play your natural shot and get the ball on the green." There's a time for fancy stuff; there are shots in the woods, out of the rough, over a pond, through the wind, that *demand* the fancy stuff, all the tricks in your bag. But whenever you can, stick with your plain-Jane shot. People would ask Sam Snead, "Sam, how do you play such-and-such shot?" And Sam would answer, "The simplest way I know how."

HALF-SPEED

A month before my father died, he gave me a copy of *How to Feel a Real Golf Swing,* with certain passages of the book highlighted with a yellow marker. I thought I might share with you one passage he marked that I think is particularly useful:

> *Whenever you hit balls, hit some shots in slow motion, a method many world-class athletes use to refine technique. Sprinter Carl Lewis still runs at half speed to analyze and improve his near-perfect style. In golf, slow motion may be your key to greater power. When he was a teenager, Davis's son, Davis Love III, asked his father how to hit the ball longer. Davis suggested his son make full-length, slow-motion swings using a driver, while not allowing the ball to travel more than 50 yards. When young Davis could hit those 50-yard drives solid and straight, he graduated to 100-yard drives—still in slow motion. In 50-yard increments Davis III worked his way up to 300 yards. Today he can drive a ball 350 yards when he wants to.*

A REAL ROUND OF GOLF

My father didn't believe much in the American practice of taking mulligans, and neither do I. If a round of golf is important to you, you should find the time to properly loosen up and hit balls before you begin, and if you do that, then you really shouldn't need the mulligan. If you're playing a round that you're going to submit for handicap purposes, you're cheating yourself if you take a mulligan, since the rules don't allow for it; with a mulligan, your score is artificially low, and therefore so is your handicap, and I don't think anybody benefits from having a vanity handicap. I always keep track of my score and I always hole all my putts, even if I'm playing by myself. Every so often, my opening shot is so awful I take a mulligan myself. Usually, I later regret it. When I'm done, I don't feel like I've played a real round of golf.

AS THE SHOULDERS TURN

To hit the ball as far as you can, you don't need a big hip turn, as many people seem to think. In fact, your lower body doesn't need to do much at all. But one thing you must do, according to my father, was make a 90-degree shoulder turn. If your left shoulder is facing due north at address, it must face due east at the top of the backswing; the left shoulder must get behind the ball. It is the shoulder turn that creates arc, and it's arc that creates distance. If you don't have the flexibility to turn your shoulder 90 degrees, you should consider doing some exercises to make your body more supple and flexible. My father was not particularly flexible, but he knew flexibility would be critical to my success, and he introduced me to flexibility experts at every turn.

WHEN YOU DON'T NEED A PRO

When I was growing up in Georgia there was an excellent junior golfer named Peter Persons who was four years older than me.

Peter's father was a very successful businessman whom everyone called Pink, and one day Pink Persons drove over to the practice tee at Sea Island in a gigantic black Cadillac, marched up to my father with Peter trudging unhappily behind him and said, "I want you to make my kid a better golfer." Dad said, "Well, let's see what the kid can do." So Peter took out a 7-iron and started drilling shots at the metal 150-yard marker. The first one missed the marker by about a yard to the left. The second was about a yard to the right. The third hit it dead on. Dad looked at Pink and said, "So what exactly is it that you want me to do with him?" Everybody got a good laugh from that. In the years since then, Peter, who plays on the tour today, has become a very close friend to everyone in my family. When he comes to Sea Island today, he still stays with my mom, and he was one of my dad's favorite pupils ever. But there was a point behind my father's crack, too: Sometimes when your game is going well there's no need to see a pro and make changes. Just enjoy the game.

CHAPTER 3

The Day Dad Fired Me

I'm the first to admit that my father and I did not have a normal, conventional relationship. It isn't often that a father and his grown son spend as much time together as my father and I did. He was my best friend; he was my teacher; *sometimes* I felt he was my boss. I think all parents are interested in the professional lives of their children, but in our case my golf career was as important to him as it was to me. This, of course, is not ordinary. Once I got out on tour, I saw other players managing just fine without calling their father after every round and giving every detail of every shot, but that was our custom. "Give me the blow-by-blow," my father would say into the mouthpiece of a pay telephone, off somewhere at a golf school, and for the next 20 minutes I'd do all the talking. When I was done he would say, "Well, you were one swing away from shooting 67," and then he'd diagnose my problems from a thousand miles away. *Try keeping your right knee more flexed. Never take the flagstick out on a downhill chip. There's no rule of etiquette that says you have to talk to your playing partner. We'll talk about it more when we're both home.* Most of the time, he was exactly right. Every so often, he wasn't.

One day, after my rookie season in 1986 and before I won my

first event in April 1987, my father and I were both home. We were on the practice tee at Sea Island, as usual. I was starting to realize that other guys, when they weren't on tour, were going hunting or fishing or fooling with their cars or their motorcycles or their boats, or spending time with their children and their wives. Or doing nothing. But here I was, on the practice tee again with Dad, off by ourselves, away from the crowd.

On this day we were talking about the position of the shaft of the club at the top of the swing. I was always worried about that, that my club shaft was not parallel to the target line. I really admired the players who worked with Hank Haney, like Mark O'Meara, because they had the most beautiful position at the top of the swing. I'd say, "Let's go see Hank Haney and see how he gets his guys into that position." And my father would say, "Sure, if he's got something good, let's use it." Dad was like that, very open as a teacher to taking good ideas from anybody and discarding the parts he thought made no sense. Curtis Strange once joked that he was so lost with his swing he was taking swing tips from Delta skycaps. Well, Dad would listen to Delta skycaps. He said you never know where genius might be lurking. But when it came to the position of the club shaft at the top of my swing, my father was just not worried; he felt the position of the club shaft at the top of the backswing was of overrated importance. He'd tell my caddies that if I ever asked on the golf course about the club-shaft position at the top, and I often did, to say it looked just fine, that any other answer would screw me up worse.

But on this particular day I was feeling rebellious. My father was an exceedingly patient teacher, and I usually was a student very willing to listen. But on this day I found myself saying to my father, "No." I wasn't willing to try things his way; I didn't want to listen to him. I wanted to do things my way; I wanted *him* to listen to *me*. We were arguing, and we had never argued. I mean *never*.

"Listen," Dad said, "I just want you to try something here."

"No, I'm not going to do that. That's stupid."

He was one of the best golf teachers in the nation. I was one of the most promising players in the nation. Each of us had egos, of course, but one of the secrets to the success of our relationship was that we held them in check. Right then, though, we were having a stand-off, low-voiced but red-faced.

"I'm trying to help you find what's missing," he said.

"I know what's missing."

He stared me down. He was fuming.

"If that's your attitude, fine. Find somebody else to teach you. Figure it out on your own." And he turned around and walked off the tee and started walking home.

Nothing like this had ever happened to us before. I couldn't get any air in my lungs. My throat was dry. I was shaking. All sorts of crazy scenarios were racing through my head. I know a scene like this may not sound like much to most people, but our relationship was not common in any way. I mean, I can only think of one time—*once*—when he really raised his voice at me. That was back in Atlanta, when I was 11 years old. I was trying to work on some very basic math problem, although math never came very easily to me. My father, on the other hand, had an incredible head for numbers, could do arithmetic in his head as if he were reciting the days of the week. I was getting very frustrated, kicking the table I was working at and throwing up my hands. He said, "Let me help you." And I must have said something like, "I don't want any help, I just can't do it." I started crying. That's when he got mad—not because I was crying, because I was giving up. He said something like, "*Never* tell me you can't do something." He was yelling. I think he must have really regretted it, because as best I can remember he never raised his voice in real anger again. Even when I did incredibly stupid things—drove drunk, wrecked a car (didn't hurt anybody, thank God)—he did not express his disappointment in a loud or angry voice. He knew what was effective and what was not.

I can still today feel the incredible sense of desperation that swept over me as I saw my father's slightly stooped back walking away from me, his shoulders sagging, his sky blue bucket hat perched on his head as it always was. In some ways, I feel like I know more now about what I was thinking than I did then. My anger didn't simply come from nowhere, so what was the root of it? Did I feel that my father was just too involved in my professional life?

All my life there have been people saying, "Well *of course* he's going to be a great golfer. His dad's a golf pro. He's got free lessons whenever he wants them. He's got access to courses and range balls all the time. He gets the best equipment. Who couldn't become a great golfer if all that was handed to you?" Naturally, there was an element of truth to those comments, but they hurt nonetheless. People who said those things had no idea of how much effort I put into my golf. They had no idea how much effort my father put into my game. Still, in some ways I was envious of friends of mine like Nick Faldo and Freddy Couples who didn't come from golfing families and still achieved considerable things in the game.

My father was so involved in my career it was, in some ways, comical. It even extended to whom I hired as my caddie. Or maybe I should say, it extended *especially* to the question of my caddie.

When I first got on tour, Dad told me I'd have to find a really good caddie, somebody I could work with week in and week out, and that I'd have to pay whatever it took to keep the caddie. He was amazed, and extremely pleased, when I told him that Herman Mitchell would be on my bag.

Herman was, and is, a famous caddie because of his girth—when he's slim he's 260 pounds or so—and because of his long partnership with Lee Trevino. But in 1986 and 1987, my first two years on tour, Trevino wasn't playing the tour much at all; he was getting himself ready for the senior tour and doing some television announcing. Herman let it be known that he'd like to work for me. I was thrilled. I told my father and *he* was thrilled; he knew what Herman had done for Lee over the years. Herman was a legend. Then my father got to know the man behind the legend.

In my sophomore year, at the Disney World Classic, Herman was on the bag and Dad was following us around. But Herman was having stomach problems—he had a lot of health problems because of his weight—and every time he'd see a bathroom he was off and running. Herman was just leaving me with a couple of clubs, running off with the bag and parking it outside the bathroom while he disappeared. If he left me with the right clubs I was fine. If he left me with the wrong ones I'd manufacture some way to hit the shot. And my dad was really getting mad, saying, "This is ridiculous, you're out here playing for your livelihood and you don't even have your clubs at your side." So, with Herman in yet another bathroom, my father opened the door, grabbed the yardage book from him, grabbed my enormous pro bag from outside the door, came charging over to where I was in the fairway—jumping over a gallery rope in his tennis shoes and polyester pants and striped shirt and light-blue bucket hat like he was an Olympic hurdler—and declared himself, straight-faced, to be my new looper.

So now he was standing with me on a par-5 with a pond in front of the green. Dad had his nose in the yardage book, trying to make sense of the thing. I said, "We've got 230 to clear the water, 242 to the hole, 3-iron."

He started fiddling with the cover to my 3-wood.

"Not 3-wood, 3-*iron*," I said.

"You laying up?"

"No, I'm not laying up," I said, and I pulled the club.

Dad was dumbfounded. He knew, of course, exactly how long I was, but it's one thing to see it on the practice tee and another to see it in a real tournament situation with real consequences if you don't pull the shot off. I hit the shot fine, hole high, 25 feet for eagle. Just then, Herman came back. My father dropped the bag at his feet. "I'm not prepared for this," he said. "You guys can have each other."

Later he said to me, "I think the world of Herman. But if his health is having an effect on your game, then he shouldn't be caddying for you, for his sake and yours." I knew all that to be true—but I was getting to a point where I would have liked to have made that decision for myself.

It was very hard for me to start declaring my independence, even though I was married, even though I would soon be a father. I was conflicted. I wanted Dad's blessing, but I wanted to make decisions for myself. I've always been interested in cars, and when I first started to make a little money I had a dream about buying a Porsche. Naturally, I asked my father about it. "Let's make a list," he said. Out came the legal pad.

"Can you afford the car?"

"Is the insurance prohibitively expensive?"

"Will you drive it safely?"

"Will all the time you spend with the car interfere with your practice?"

"Does it make sense to buy it now, with Robin pregnant?"

"Is it something you really want?"

The answers were sort of, yes, probably not, yes, no and definitely yes.

"Well if it's something you really want, you should get it for yourself," he said. "It's important to reward yourself."

We went through similar lines of questioning about whether I was putting away enough money for a "rainy day." And whether playing in corporate outings for $1,000 on Mondays after tournaments was a good use of my time. And whether flying overseas in December to play in a tournament in South Africa was really good for my golf game. And whether I was sleeping eight hours at night. And whether I was still eating junk food on the road. And whether I was doing my stretching exercises. And whether I was doing this, doing that, whatever.

And then one day, the way these things happen, it just boiled over on the practice tee at Sea Island, with me telling Dad that I would not try it his way and him telling me to figure it out myself and him walking off, heading for home, his curving back getting smaller and smaller with every step, while my eyes welled up with tears.

My first thought was, "OK, I *will* find another teacher." And after that, "What have I done now?" And after that, "What will I do now?" My head was just bombarded with thoughts. *Have I done irreparable damage to our relationship? Can he really quit on me like this? I'm going to be lost without him. Are people looking at me? Did they see Dad storm off?* I was just standing there, having no idea what to do next, for what was up to then the longest five minutes of my life.

My father walked all the way to our house and then he started coming back.

I said, "I'm so sorry."

He said, "I am, too."

"We're putting too much pressure on ourselves," I said.

"It's just so hard for me to find ways to improve your game when you're playing at the level you are," he said.

"I should have found other words to say what I wanted to say."

"I should have paid attention to my own rule: 'I get a vote, Davis gets a vote, and Davis's body gets a vote.' And your body was saying that you most definitely did not want to try what I was proposing."

I think it was that moment when I learned, when I really understood for the first time, the *depth* of the effort my father had put into me, and how that effort was a total expression of his love for me and his dreams for me. Nothing more and nothing less. And I think that's when he realized that his boy had become a man. A few weeks after that day on the practice tee, I won my first tournament, with Herman Mitchell on the bag and my father far off at a golf school.

WHAT YOU NEED TO KNOW

My father taught me to play by "feel," but he didn't mean by that to take the science out of the game. I know amateurs—no touring professional would dare do this—who think the "true" way to play the game is to just eyeball the distance, grab a club, and play. I'm all for fast play, but I would never want to hit a shot without knowing the precise distance I need to play the shot. I know exactly how far I hit each club under normal conditions, and then I make adjustments accordingly. Conditions are not just rain and wind or whether your ball is going uphill or downhill or the quality of your lie, but the quality of your mind, how your body is feeling, whether you are nervous or tired, and what that is going to do to the distance you hit the ball. All that is playing by feel. But the first, necessary, calculated part is knowing how far you hit each club, and so many golfers just don't know. They know how far their best 7-iron will go; they can give you every detail about the time they bent one around an oak, over an evergreen, and onto the back tier of a green. But the important question is this: How far does your average shot, allowing for a less than perfect strike, go? That's what you need to know.

FORGIVE YOURSELF

Anyone who has been around the game for a while knows golf is cruel, that golf is punishing, that golf is hard, that the rules are unforgiving. Golf is a game in which you have to play your mistakes. Given all that, my father could never understand why golfers were so hesitant to forgive themselves on the golf course. You see players making a lousy shot, then they literally hit themselves on the head. Is this sane behavior? I don't think so. "Learn to forgive yourself," Dad used to say. You might as well, because nobody else will. And if you don't forgive yourself after a bad shot, your chances on the next one are quickly diminished.

SLOW DOWN

In the long history of golf, there has probably never been a player who did not rush his swing from time to time. Even my friend Fred Couples, for all his laconic ease and graceful nonchalance, will swing too hard and too fast once a year or so. My father would say to me, "Davis, do me a favor. Be the first student I've ever had who is *not* in a rush to finish his backswing." When I get going too fast, and we all do, I try to remember those words. And when that's not enough, I call on another thought he'd use to slow golfers down: After you make the backswing, *feel* the change in direction before you begin the downswing. Be aware that you are changing directions. It won't work forever—the hyper person especially will always fight the tendency to swing too fast—but it will work for a while. And when it wears out, you can always go back to the first thought.

PRACTICE WITH A PURPOSE

Dad was a huge believer in the value of practice, but he didn't prescribe the kind of rote practice that some golfers, including Lee Trevino and Ben Hogan, believe in. Trevino will spend all day hitting balls, hitting as many as 500 some days, just grooving his swing and grooving it some more. My father thought most golfers got more out of shorter sessions if they had definite goals in mind. He'd like to hear a golfer say to himself, for example, "Today I'm going to practice hitting my mid-irons higher," then do all the things necessary to achieve that goal. Of course, my father wouldn't say, "I'm going to work on hitting the ball higher." He'd say, "I'm going to *practice* hitting the ball higher." Practice can be fun; work is work.

THE BEST TIME TO PRACTICE

I once asked my father, "Dad, what's the best time to practice?" I thought he might say, "Early in the morning." He was an early riser, and he never understood how I could, if my schedule allowed it, sleep past nine. I thought he might say, "After a lesson." But he didn't say that, either. His answer was simple and profound: "After you've played well," he said. You *don't* practice before a round; when you hit balls before playing, all you're doing is getting in the mood, oiling the joints, and seeing which way the ball's going that day. Practice after a good round and you're ingraining good habits, which is easier than breaking bad ones.

TRY LESS HARD

Most golfers just whale away on the practice tee, then they get on the golf course and get really earnest, really serious, about every shot and chip and putt. Five hours and ninetysomething strokes later, they're often frustrated and upset and ready to go back to the "driving range" and start flailing at balls again, just to vent a little anger. My father always felt it was really important to *not* try so hard on the golf course. The practice tee was the place to try things and to work hard; the golf course was the place to let things go, free yourself up. He'd say, "Don't try harder on the golf course. Try *less* hard." For some people, to whom golf is work, that's a revelation. Golf is not supposed to be work, even if you play it for a living. Practice might be considered work, at least sometimes, but not playing the game itself.

ONE SENTENCE

Sometimes my father was able to improve a pupil's game with one sentence. For instance, he'd have pupils who were able golfers but did not know how to address the ball. They'd position their feet and hands and the rest of their body, then put the clubhead behind the ball. Not helpful. Always position your clubhead first, get it centered to your ball and to the target line, then move the rest of your body into a position that is defined by your clubhead position. Here's how my father reduced these thoughts to a one-sentence lesson: "All good swings flow from good stances."

BACKSWING POSITIONS

On the practice tee, at college tournaments in particular, I often see good young golfers compulsively working on their backswings, then hitting balls from a variety of different backswing positions, trying to groove a perfect swing. The work is admirable, but, my father would have said, misguided. He didn't like players to work on backswings on the practice tee, with a ball at the player's feet; he felt it promoted a very mechanical swing. A better approach, he felt, was to work on backswing positions in the comfort of your own home, in front of a mirror, then bring it out to the course once you have it ingrained. One note, though, about working in the house in front of a mirror: Be careful of the follow-through. Have you ever seen a steel clubhead crashing into a full-length mirror? Not a pretty sight. A lot of the furniture in my mom's house today still bears the dents from the indoor practicing my brother, father, and I did night after night.

A QUESTION OF BALANCE

A good golf teacher is, by nature, a borrower. My father borrowed ideas from scores of people, including his mentor, Harvey Penick of the Austin Country Club, and his longtime colleague, Claude Harmon, the former Masters champion who was the professional at Winged Foot. I'm sure that Harvey's son, Tinsley, and Claude's son, Butch, both well-known Texas golf pros, have borrowed ideas from my father. In the business of golf teaching, this is not known as plagiarism or theft; it's known as sharing knowledge. Bobby Jones, the great amateur, had a friend named Fred Haskins, a teaching professional in Georgia. Haskins spread word of Jones's thoughts about the game throughout the South. One of these thoughts my father was enamored of and he instilled it in me: To improve your balance, hit balls with your feet together. If you take too big a swing or too fast a swing with your feet together, you'll topple over.

MAKE PRACTICE A GAME

One of my closest friends on tour is Mike Hulbert. Mike is one of the funniest people on tour, he always has a plan for what he wants to do next and he's always going a hundred miles an hour. I like to hang out with him just to see if I can keep up. The thing about Mike that really impressed my dad was the way he practiced. He loves to practice and it's never monotonous for him because he's always making a game out of it. If you're in a practice bunker with him he'll say, "OK, first guy to hole out a bunker shot gets his dinner paid for tonight." And then we'll both stay out there a half hour, trying to be the first person to hole a bunker shot. Dad would say, "I *like* this guy."

GO FOR THE HOLE

There are some things I do in golf that my father didn't do. For instance, when I'm going really well, I feel like I'm trying to hole all my shots, or at least all my shots where I'm expecting to reach the green, an idea I first learned from Dr. Bob Rotella, my mental coach. I think that idea was too audacious for my father, maybe even too New Age. And there is a down side to it: When you *don't* hole a 200-yard shot with a 5-iron, is that now considered a disappointment? My father felt that when you had a 5-iron in your hand, your first goal should be to knock it on the green and your second goal should be to hit it close enough to have a legitimate birdie putt. There's a lot of sense in all that, but I still like the idea of trying to hole every shot. Maybe it is a little audacious, but is that so bad?

HOW FAR?

I once heard a man ask my father, "How far back do you swing the club until it starts to rise?" My father's answer was succinct: "As far as you can."

FRED COUPLES

Freddy Couples is one of my closest friends on tour. Off the course, he is as relaxed and nonchalant as he appears on TV on the course. When he comes to stay with us in our home in St. Simons, he usually leaves with his head shaking; Robin and I are always running around at home, getting Lexie off to horseback-riding lessons while Dru is in the front yard hitting golf balls in the direction of large windows, and all the while the phone's ringing off the hook. Once Freddy said to us, "You guys got *way* too much going on here." Freddy's a mellow guy, off the course.

On the course, I think he's much less relaxed than he appears to be. All the club twirling and whistling and that leisurely stroll thing he does is mostly a way for him to combat his nervousness.

I think I know his moods well, and that's one reason we were so successful as a two-man team representing the United States in the World Cup, which we won four straight years, starting in 1992. We each have the ability to pick up the other when one of us is down. And Fred takes his golf much more seriously than he would ever let you know.

One of Freddy's greatest skills is his ability to keep the game simple. That requires a certain genius. For instance, I used to routinely hit a 1-iron on the 18th hole at Augusta National. A lot of long hitters do. Then Freddy said to me, "Why would you play a club you can hit *into* the left fairway bunker when you can bust driver right over it?" The argument for hitting driver on 18 at Augusta National—and it's a subject long drivers talk about with some regularity at the Masters—was never put so plainly to me before. Thanks to Freddy's counsel, I hit driver there now, and that decision has served me well.

I think the main reason Freddy has not achieved as much in his career, at the same age, as a Raymond Floyd or a Tom Watson or a Lee Trevino is that there's only so much attention he wants or can even stand. If his back can hold up, and he decides he wants to have a career like a Floyd or a Watson or a Trevino, he will. Since announcing his engagement to Tawnya Dodd, from the back of a bus on the way to the 1995 Ryder Cup matches at Oak Hill, Fred's been very happy, and his golf has been very good.

THE KINCAID JOURNALS

Many club professionals have formidable libraries of golf books. There was one instruction book that my father did not have that I knew he coveted, a book held in almost cult-like status in certain golf circles. The book is a collection of seventeenth-century journals kept by a Scot named Thomas Kincaid. The Kincaid journals would probably be largely unknown, except that the journals were reprinted in another book called *Golf in the Making*. The Kincaid journals were the subject of a Charles Price column in *Golf Digest* in 1986 and my father clipped and saved the Price column; it was among his papers when he died. I'm sure I know why he saved it. Kincaid had insights into the swing, over three centuries ago, that have not been improved upon since. Kincaid wrote, "You must hit through the ball, not at it, with the sensation that the clubhead is still accelerating after it has made contact. This is the secret to distance. The way to perfect this sensation is to practice hitting the ball as easily as possible, then increasing the force of the swing by degrees, practicing each degree until it becomes a habit. The time will not be wasted. Perfecting each degree will teach you to play half shots, pitches and chips. The easiest degree will help perfect your putting. While increasing these degrees, never alter your posture or your pivot." Centuries later, my father was saying the same things.

BE A GOOD COACH

Have you ever heard a player say, "Nice shot, stupid"? Not to his playing partner, but to himself? Or, "You're an idiot." Or, most eloquently, "You stink." My father thought this kind of talk, which is so common in golf, was debilitating. He'd always tell me to be my own best friend on the golf course. If I'd berate myself, he'd say, "Would you talk to your best friend that way?" And I'd say, sheepishly, "No." And he'd say, "Then don't talk to yourself that way, either." On the course, I try to tell myself the things I need to hear. I try to encourage myself, explain away bad shots, praise myself for my good shots. I might as well; I know when I get off the course Robin and the kids will give me a dose of reality.

And when you're working on a new move on the practice tee, be as patient with yourself as a good coach would be. My father stressed that to me when I left college to join the tour, when he knew I wouldn't have my swing coach—my father—around that much. The tendency is to expect instant results, and to beat up on yourself if they don't come. That attitude will insure that they will never come. Be patient with yourself. Be your own best coach. If your coach wouldn't berate you, then don't do it to yourself.

GAME CONDITIONS

Dad knew that a boring practice session was a worthless practice session. He always encouraged me to simulate game conditions when practicing. If you're hitting drivers on the practice tee, you might say to yourself, "I cannot hit the ball left of that 250-yard marker. If I do, that's out of bounds." Or you might say, "OK, this is my approach shot to the first green, a 160-yard 7-iron that I want to punch low, under the wind." Doing this also teaches you anger control; you can learn how *not* to get mad at your bad shots on the practice tee, then carry that over to the course.

INCENTIVE

My father understood the power of incentive. Bribes, if you must. A lot of times, Dad and his assistant, Jimmy Hodges, and I would be on the practice tee, working on this and that. Jimmy was a great friend of mine and our conversation would often drift to which fish were biting or when bow-and-arrow season for deer was starting. We were always making plans. And Dad would say, "OK, Jimmy, Davis—give me a half-hour on buried bunker shots, and then go off and buy your chum or your slugs or whatever it is. But give me the 30 minutes first." We would, and then we'd tear out of there, visions of speckled trout or 12-point bucks running through our heads.

CHAPTER 4

On Winning and Losing

I sometimes wonder: Why do we value winning so much? Why is winning so important? Our entire culture seems devoted to separating winners from losers. Baseball teams in the World Series either win or lose. Politicians running for office either win or lose. There are bumper stickers that read, "He who dies with the most toys wins." Americans, from the day we're old enough to respond to our names, are taught that winning is good and losing is bad. If someone is successful, you'll hear people say, "He's a winner." If someone can't keep a job, you hear, "What a loser." *Sports Illustrated* tells us who wins and who loses on a weekly basis. *The Wall Street Journal* does the same thing every weekday morning. In a society dominated by sports and money, winners and losers are so easy to identify they might as well be wearing labels on their lapels. We're so bombarded by the idea that everyone can be ultimately classified as either a winner or a loser that the classification system is part of our subconscious. As a rule, we don't even think about it.

My father thought about it. His father was a man who made fortunes and lost fortunes in the oil business, and my grandfather's feelings of self-worth rose and fell with the size of his bank statements. My father saw the ridiculousness in that; I think that's one of the reasons he became so infatuated with golf, and one of the reasons he stressed to us that our feelings of self-worth should not be governed by the quality of our golf games. In golf, the only thing that really matters—this is a tired cliche but born in truth—is what you do against yourself. Have you played to the best of your capabilities? Did you enjoy yourself on the course? How did you do against par? I think having this attitude served him well in his own playing career. He never had any major successes as a tour player, he never won an event, but his satisfaction level was very high. For a short-hitting club pro he played very well. He had a sense of proportion in everything he did.

In the back of the *1996 PGA Tour Media Guide* there's a list of the 100 leaders in career earnings on the tour. Only one name has an asterisk next to it, No. 75, Bobby Wadkins. On the bottom of the page there's a notation: **=non-winner.* That offends me. It's as if the only thing important to know about Bobby's position on the career money list is that he's never won a tour event.

And yet, and yet—there's something about winning that is like no other feeling I know. It's a very difficult emotion to describe, although I suppose we've all known the feeling on some level. When you win you've done something better than everybody else. You are the subject of envy. That may not sound very charitable, but it's true. That's why you hear so many runners-up say in press-tent interviews, "If I couldn't win the tournament, I'm glad my friend Sammy Sansabelt could." Envy is such a motivating emotion that people were surprised when I said, speaking of Freddy Couples's win at the 1992 Masters with total earnestness, "I'm as happy he won the Masters as if I'd won it myself."

Probably the nicest thing about winning is the adulation, being the center of attention. Of course, some people think they want to be the center of attention, then when they get there they find they don't like it so much. I have friends on the tour who are genuinely uninterested in being the center of attention, and their record reflects it. For all their skill, they don't win. Or, having won, they decide, "This is not worth it." I happen to love being the center of attention. I guess that's why I started practicing signing my autograph at a young age.

Through the end of the 1996 season I've won 10 tour events, and in some ways the first one was the most memorable. A first win is like first love: fresh and new and exciting. My inaugural win came in 1987, in my second year on the tour. As a rookie in 1986 I had a chance to win the Canadian Open, but my inexperience cost me. In the final round, on the par-5 fifth hole, I made bogey by trying to reach a green when I should have laid up. Even worse, I tried to make up for it on the next hole by hitting driver where I'd been hitting 1-iron all week, and drove into the rough, leading to another bogey. The first mistake was bad, but not sticking to my gameplan because I'd messed up was much, much worse. I played like a rookie, and I finished third; the winner was Bob Murphy, a wily veteran who played like a veteran coming in.

In the first three months of my sophomore season, I played well; I was in contention several times, but still no wins. By April, I had played in about 40 tour events and I was starting to wonder when my first victory would come, but I wasn't obsessed by the idea. I wasn't obsessed by it because my father wasn't; he knew that if you took care of the things you can take care of, the winning would take care of itself. But as I headed to Hilton Head for the Heritage Classic, I was conscious of how good and valuable a win would be: a two-year exemption from tour qualifying; a $117,000 payday; an automatic invitation to next year's Masters and the World Series of Golf and the Tournament of Champions. Robin and I were living in a condominium at the time; a six-figure payday would mean we were well on our way to a house.

Hilton Head—tour players usually refer to a tournament by its location, not its official name—always comes the week after the Masters, and in 1987 I didn't play at Augusta. (I hadn't met any of the requirements necessary to earn an invitation.) In those days, the tour stop before Augusta was the Greater Greensboro Open, and I was really irritated with myself when I discovered, shortly before the start of the GGO, that I had forgotten to sign up for the tournament before the cut-off date. I wanted to play in the GGO chiefly because if I won it I would receive an invitation to the Masters. Rather than take two weeks off, I decided to play in a little tournament held opposite the Masters, the Magnolia Classic, held in Hattiesburg, Mississippi. I didn't play well—I remember Nick Faldo shot four consecutive 67s for second place, behind David Ogrin—but I had a wonderful week, much of which I spent with my father's mother and other relatives who lived in Hattiesburg.

After Hattiesburg, I went home for a day and had a terrific lesson with Jack Lumpkin, who was at Sea Island for a *Golf Digest* School. It was an unusual lesson because Jack seldom gave me any advice directly; usually, if he had an observation he told it to my father, who would filter it and then pass it along to me if he thought it had merit. But on this occasion, Dad told Jack to tell it to me directly. Jack wanted me to keep my left arm closer to my body, and when I did I started hitting the ball very well. Then Jimmy Hodges gave me a putter out of the pro shop that he thought I'd like; I took a few putts with it on the practice green and I fell in love with it, put it right in the bag. That was odd for me because I usually like to stick with a putter through thick and thin.

My father and I drove up to Hilton Head from Sea Island. I loved spending time with him like that, when it was so relaxed and there weren't any other people around and all we could do was talk, or not talk. When we arrived at Hilton Head, I spent part of a day with an old friend and colleague of my father's, Peter Kostis, who was then known principally for his teaching and is now probably better known for his announcing on television. Peter can be a tough and grizzled guy, and the nice thing about that is that when he pays you a compliment you know he really means it. So when he said to me, "Man, are you hitting it pure," it really stuck with me.

My father saw the practice tee at tour events as a great place to test clubs and talk to people and relax—and a terrible place to practice. He suggested we go over to another club, Long Cove, where his friend Jim Ferree was the head professional. Jim, who later became an accomplished player on the senior tour, watched me for a while and he said the same things Peter Kostis and the others were saying. I knew they all really meant it. It's amazing what feelings of confidence will do for your golf game. People were kidding me about how poorly suited Harbour Town, a gem of a course designed by Pete Dye, was for my game; the course is short by tour standards, and really tight, and the greens are small. In theory, Harbour Town should not be a natural home for a power game like mine. But theories don't mean a thing when you've got your game together.

On Wednesday, my pro-am team and I won with a comically low score, 51, or 20 under par. So that was a nice start and it also meant $750 for me. Now that I'm a so-called tour star I sometimes find myself thinking that I don't feel like spending five hours on a Wednesday playing in a pro-am for a relatively meager amount of money. When I start to feel that way, I try to remind myself of what it was like in 1987 when I was quite delighted to have an extra $750. (And if I don't remind myself, Robin is sure to remind me.) I also try to remember that the amateurs—those playing on Wednesdays, those coming to the tournaments, those who watch on TV, those who buy the clubs that bear our names—literally make our livelihoods possible. Any player who forgets, and we all do from time to time, is a fool.

The first round I shot 70, which I felt was pretty solid. Then I looked at the leaderboard and saw that Mark Hayes had shot 64. I was already six shots out of the lead and I hadn't played a poor shot yet! I remember thinking, "Damn, this is a tough crowd out here." It's sort of like the high-school valedictorian who goes to a Duke or a Stanford or a Harvard. In high school, that kid is *the* brain, nobody can touch him, everybody is in awe of his brilliance. Then at Duke, *everybody* was the valedictorian of their high-school class. You realize that you're not so special. In that situation, some people will ask themselves, "OK, what do I have to do to distinguish myself?" And others will say, "I guess I'm just part of the pack now." Same thing happens on tour.

In the second round at Hilton Head that year, I shot 67, while Hayes, who was an excellent putter and a very precise player, shot 68. Still five shots back. In Saturday's third round—moving day, we call it, the day you either move into contention or drift so far down that come Sunday you're just playing for a paycheck—I had another 67. By this point, Steve Jones and Gene Sauers had taken over the lead at 13 under par. They had played three rounds in 200 strokes. I thought that was phenomenal, because I knew how well I had performed to play them in 204 shots. I was four shots back, and I knew I wasn't out of it. My father and I were staying together that week, and I was really disappointed on Sunday morning when he had to leave to go to a *Golf Digest* School. That's how it always was then; Dad and I would spend great chunks of time together, and then he'd be off to teach at another school. Every so often when we were together for long periods I grew to resent him, because he was *so* fascinated by golf and so consumed with my improvement that I felt suffocated—but that was rare. More often, the time we spent together, like that week at Hilton Head, was just so special, and I'm so lucky that I can look back at that week, almost a decade later, and know how happy we were and how much we both appreciated the time.

I shot a final-round 67 and won the tournament by a shot. This time, unlike my final round at the Canadian Open the year before, I was more patient, calmer; I hit 1-irons off the tee pretty much all week, and I stuck with that strategy on Sunday. Also, my father had worked with me on knockdowns and punch shots, knowing I'd need them at Harbour Town; I had confidence in those shots, and they were there when I needed them in that final round. Steve Jones, who was in the last group of the day, had a chance to win the tournament with a par on the last hole, the beautiful seaside par-4 with the lighthouse beyond the green, but his tee shot went out of bounds and he made six. I felt horrible for him, but being a winner was an awesome feeling regardless. After that, I always had a soft spot in my heart for Steve; when I was away from the tour and looking at scores in the paper, I'd always make note of how Steve was playing. That doesn't mean I wanted Steve to win the 1996 U.S. Open. I wanted to be the guy hugging my wife and children on the 18th green. But it does mean I was truly happy for him, almost as happy for him as I would have been had I won myself.

The thing I remember best about the last round was what Herman Mitchell, my caddie at the time, said to me on the 18th tee. I had nailed my tee shot, long and straight, and Herman said, "That-away to drive it, Babe." You could hear it on TV. He was so calm and reassuring. I remember thinking, "I am so lucky to have this guy on my bag."

Herman did so much for my game, both that week and over the

course of the year or two we were together. He has a very great understanding of the game, very simple but very great, particularly the mental side of it and how to manage a player. If he saw me eyeing my driver on a hole where he wanted me to hit 1-iron, he'd say, "Don't you be even *thinking* about the driver now." On one hole I couldn't get the read of the putt and I said to Herman, "Split the right edge?" And he said, "Ain't nothing but the center of the hole." He eliminated a lot of doubt and taught me how to relax on the golf course. He had a wonderful memory for what the wind had been doing in previous rounds and he was an excellent player himself, a superb hustler because he certainly didn't look like a guy who could play scratch golf, not with all that girth, but he could.

Because of his size, and a bad heart, Herman walked as little as he possibly could. Yes, for as long as he was on the bag he was forever giving me a driver as I came off a green, and then he'd be gone. But he knew how to call clubs and he knew how to calm nerves. Herman had so much to do with my winning my first title, and Herman was on the bag only because he and Lee Trevino liked and respected my father and they generously extended those feelings to me.

A few days after my first win I received a letter from my father. It read:

Dear Davis,

Our travel plans have kept us apart since your win, but I have thought about it often and wanted to talk with you, to tell you how proud I was of how *you won, how you displayed maturity far beyond your age, how your conduct told all of us who were watching that you felt sorry for Steve, but that you were preparing to go extra holes if he made five.*

Your golf shots showed me that there will be more wins, that you wanted to hit those shots under pressure, that you liked *being in the hunt. Some don't. You belong there.*

My hat is off to your courage—and to your composure.

Much love,
Dad

Of all the pages of writing I have from my father, that's the one I prize the most.

SWING THOUGHTS

I'm sometimes asked, "What do you think about when you're making a swing?" In answering, I know I'm quoting my father: "Ideally, nothing." This is not always possible; some days—many days, even—you need a little brain trigger to get your swing going. That's what a swing thought, or a tip, is all about. But on your best days, there's not a thing in your head. When my father would start with a new student, the first thing he would have the student do is to throw a ball into my father's open hand. Underhand, overhand, hard, soft—any way they wanted to throw it. The vast majority of students could get the ball right into my father's hand because they weren't thinking a single thing. No mechanics.

Remember Chevy Chase's brilliant advice in *Caddyshack?* He tells his playing partner, "Be the ball." There's a lot in that. My brother, Mark, is a good amateur golfer, a scratch player who can beat me more than occasionally. When he putts, no matter from what distance, he doesn't look at the ball, he looks at the hole. He's taken the ball-throwing principle to its next logical step. The goal is the target; by focusing only on the target, as the beginning student would focus only on my father's cupped hands, you block out all the stray thoughts. The next step after that is to "be the ball."

LONG BUNKER SHOTS

Here are my father's suggestions for how to play long bunker shots:

1. Take an extra club.
2. Dig in, but not too deep.
3. Choke up as much as you dig in.
4. Play the ball farther back in your stance—not more forward, as many suggest.
5. Pick the ball clean.
6. Make a full swing, being sure to accelerate through the ball.
7. Look at your divot.

MAKE IT ROUTINE

Jack Nicklaus slowed golf down, but improved the quality of play, with his preshot routine: Lining up the shot from behind the ball, picking out a spot to which he wanted to follow through, imagining the flight of the ball. Before Nicklaus, nobody talked much about routine, but now everybody who is serious about the game has developed some sort of preshot routine. The critical thing is to have the routine, like the swing, become part of your muscle memory. My father would say, "A routine is not a routine if you have to think about it." Practice your routine until it becomes part of you.

OVERCOMING DOUBT

I can still hear some of my father's favorite quotations in my head, and I'm sure I always will. One of the things he was fond of saying was, "Doubt is the number one cause of missed shots." There's a lot in that. If you can get rid of the doubt, you significantly increase your chances of not missing the shot. So how do you get rid of doubt? Practice, for one thing. If you've played the shot successfully in practice, then you can play it on the course. Knowledge, for another. If you know your ordinary 6-iron will go 165 yards and that's how far you need to hit a shot to carry a pond, then you know you have the correct club. And a sense of proportion, for another. Doubt is usually a function of attaching too much significance to a shot in the first place. Hey, even when you're playing for your livelihood, even when you're playing for a national title, golf is still only a game. Don't doubt, enjoy! I know I don't always look like the happiest golfer in the world, but deep down inside, I am. I *love* what I do. I play golf! What is there to doubt?

CHANGE SPEEDS

To teach me balance and control of my own power, my father would have me hit balls with full swings that were one-quarter normal speed, one-half normal speed, and three-quarters normal speed. If you can hit quality shots at those different speeds, then you're in control of your golf swing. But that doesn't mean that on the golf course you try to vary your distances by varying your swing speeds. As a general rule, on the course you should have one basic swing speed, from driver through wedge. If you need to hit the ball a shorter distance than normal for that club, shorten the backswing.

MORE PLEASING WITH WOOD

In my early years on the tour, there were still quite a few players on the tour using drivers made of wood. Greg Norman, Tom Kite, Ben Crenshaw, Tom Watson, Jack Nicklaus, Fred Couples, me—a lot of guys. Although my father was a traditionalist who loved the whole art behind how a wooden club was made, he was also a believer in technology. He fiddled with metal drivers himself. He said to me, "If you ever find a metal driver that you can hit better than your Cleveland Classic, don't be afraid to make a change. But don't make a change just because everybody else is." Well, I'm still hitting my wooden driver. In fact, I'm about the only guy left on tour hitting a wooden driver, along with Justin Leonard.

The Cleveland has been in my bag since 1985. It was given to me by a good friend, Bob Spence. I experiment with metal drivers often; I find—for me, and not necessarily for you—they go marginally longer than my wooden driver, but they don't give me any *shape.* I find it more difficult to create a shape to my drives off the metal face, which is important to me. Golf holes are seldom perfectly straight; hitting a tee shot with some curve to it helps me get into the demands of the hole. I also love the sound my ball makes as it comes off the persimmon insert of my driver.

I'm no technophobe. My fairway "woods" have metal heads. I'd use graphite shafts if I thought I could hit the ball straighter with them. (I don't.) But when it comes to my old wooden driver, I guess the only thing I can really say is that I enjoy golf more with it, and I think I play better with it. I have no doubt that my father would back my decision to stay with wood 100 percent. In fact, I can imagine wood making a little comeback someday. Golf is somehow more *pleasing* to me when played with a driver made of wood.

KEEP YOUR GRIPS DRY

If you're playing on a wet day and you're carrying more than one club as you go off to play a shot, don't put the other clubs on the moist ground. Once a grip gets wet, it's hard to get it really dry again. What my father would do is put a tee in the ground and rest the end of the grip on the top of the tee. Dry grips make for better golf. Heck, Ben Crenshaw lost a chance to win a Masters because his grip was wet and it slipped in his hands as he played a shot on the 72nd hole of the tournament. That was more of a towel issue—he didn't have a dry one by the end of the day—but the point is this: anything you can do to keep your grips dry is helpful. The tee method is foolproof.

A ONCE-IN-A-LIFETIME SHOT

This idea my father borrowed from Jack Nicklaus—whose name is usually written, and understandably so, as *the great* Jack Nicklaus. (The only other golfer I know who consistently gets that treatment, and deserves it, is Bobby Jones: *the great* Bobby Jones.) Nicklaus often says, and my father often repeated, "Try your best on every shot." That may seem obvious, but all of us, myself included, fail to live up to that ideal from time to time. Nicklaus has such immense respect for the game that he is consciously aware, with every shot he plays, *that he will never again have the chance to play that shot.* So since every shot is a once-in-a-lifetime proposition, you owe it to yourself to make the most of it. There's another way of looking at it, too: Every shot you hit is a shot closer to the last shot you're ever going to play. Some may find that a bit morbid, but it's the truth. With that thought in mind, there is meaning attached to every swing you make.

THE WORDS OF GOLF

My father felt that two golfers could never be strangers because they shared such a strong common bond, and part of that bond was the language distinct to golf. Dad never sat me down and taught me golf "grammar;" it was just something I picked up. Whenever I hear somebody use the word *trap* for *bunker,* I know I'm speaking to somebody recently arrived. My father was a definite *bunker* man. Also, he used *flagstick,* where so many others use *pin.* He preferred *cup* to *hole.* He never used golf as a verb, as in, "I golf with my wife on Sunday afternoons in November." He avoided the gerund form, too: "Joe didn't come to work today—he's golfing." (Though when he would say, "That man can golf his ball," it was a definite compliment, meaning he could play the game deftly, with subtlety and skill.) He'd cringe, at least internally, if he heard somebody say, "How'd you shoot today?" That question should be posed as, "What did you shoot today?" Or, "How did you play today?" The former question, in many amateur circles, is considered bad form; the question is too personal. If the score is good, the answer will come with the latter question; if it doesn't, then the person you're speaking with doesn't want you to know. Dad loved golf in the British Isles, and he passed that enthusiasm down to me; just for fun he'd use British golf phrases from time to time: *al-*

batross for *eagle, trolley* for *pull cart.* Sometimes he'd use *practice field* for the American *driving range,* which really suggests the wrong idea altogether. But if he wanted to know somebody's handicap, he was pure Texas: "What can he shoot?"

A COLD-WEATHER TIP

When you're walking to a green with your putter in hand on a cold day, don't carry it by the shaft with your bare hands. The steel gets cold, then your hands get cold, then you lose your putting touch. Keep your hands in your pockets and carry the putter in the crook of your arm. I'm not sure where my father picked that one up—probably by playing in the British Open. In the British Isles, they take a very sensible approach to golf. I find I always pick up something interesting about the game when I'm there. Like their term for even par: They call it *level.* That really says it all, don't you think?

A TEACHER'S GOAL

Not long before my father died, he and his old, close colleague Paul Runyan had a long, interesting conversation about how the game is taught. The conversation was moderated by Jerry Tarde, the editor of *Golf Digest,* and a transcript of the conversation was among my father's papers when I began to assemble my thoughts, and my father's thoughts, for this book. Paul and my father were talking about what a teacher can and cannot do for a pupil. My father said, "I've told Davis that his job with me is to make me obsolete. He doesn't need to do that in a hurry, but at some point, if he's going to be a great player, he will have to take total responsibility for his winning."

CHAPTER 5

On the Road to Waycross

My father was sensitive to the fact that not everyone in the world was as fascinated by golf as he was. He tried to show a curiosity for other people's hobbies, but it never took him long to steer the conversation back to where he wanted it. For instance, he was always careful to show an interest in my mother's gardening. A typical conversation:

Dad: "Hey, Penta, how's your corn coming this year?

Mom: "Good, Davis."

Dad: "Glad to hear it. You want to go play golf this afternoon?"

Other times the conversation would go this way:

Dad: "Say, Penta, how are your tomatoes coming along?"

Mom: "Were you looking to play nine holes or 18?"

One November day at the end of the 1988 golf season, near the start of the duck-hunting season, I was about to get in my truck to make the hour's drive over to Waycross, Georgia, to pick up a new motor for my boat. As I was getting ready to leave, my father showed up and asked if he could come along. I said sure. I liked going on rides with Dad—as long as I did the driving. (Dad's driving was horrendous. He'd get so wrapped up in what he was saying he'd pay almost no attention to his driving. His speed would go up and down so much you could get sick with him behind the wheel.) He jumped into the passenger seat of the truck's tall cab; even at age 53, he was still very light on his feet.

"So what kind of engine are you getting?" dad asked.

"Johnson," I said. I knew my answer would not be meaningful to him. Johnson, Evinrude, Mercury, they were all the same to him.

"Good engine, isn't it?"

I was curious to see how long he could go before turning the conversation to the subject I knew he wanted to talk about.

My 1988 season had been awful. In 1987, as a sophomore on the tour, I had won at Hilton Head, finished 33rd on the money list, showed improvement in all parts of my game. In 1988 I finished 75th on the money list, didn't win, wasn't even in contention for anything. I missed the cut in the Masters, the U.S. Open, and the British Open, and I didn't even qualify for the PGA Championship. I was disqualified—I actually disqualifed myself—from the Players Championship because I putted with a putter that became bent over the course of the round. (The rules require a bent club to be taken out of play.) Herman, having reunited with Lee Trevino on the senior tour, was off the bag and I missed him. I wasn't getting anything out of my practice, which made me not *want* to practice. Lexie had been born in June, so when I was on the road I was always thinking about what was going on at home, and when I was at home all I wanted to do was help Robin out and spend time with Lexie. If I had any free time, I wanted to hunt or fish or fool around with cars. We were thinking about building a house and I was running around a lot, making extra checks where I could in Monday outings and pro-ams and long-drive contests. I knew what was coming from Dad. At least, I thought I did. We always had a season-end review in November, going back to high school. We'd talk about what I had done in the previous year and what my goals would be for the new year and what I, or we, would have to do to reach them. They were fun conversations because they were always about the future, about getting better. They were filled with optimism. This one was not.

"I'm wondering if you're enjoying the game as much as you used to."

His words threw me. He had never said anything like that to me before.

"Of course I am." Thinking about my reply now, nearly a decade later, I'm not certain if that answer was wholly candid. I've discovered over the years that my underlying love for the game is unwavering, but my week-to-week passion to do all the things you need to do to be competitive on the PGA Tour is subject to mood swings. I didn't know that then, and even if I had known it, I could never have admitted it to myself, or to my father. To say the words, "Dad, sometimes golf feels like a job,"—that was a sentence I could never say. After all, the chief goal of my father's teaching was for golf to *never* feel like a job. A lofty goal when your student is a touring professional, and not always attainable.

"Well, I hope you are," Dad said. His words hung there in the cool air of the cab. I wondered, where was he going with this?

"I hope you're not playing just to make money. You'll always be able to make money. You can make money on your talent alone. I just hope you still love the competition."

"Of course I do."

"Because there are so many distractions out there today. The shoot-outs and the pro-ams and the manufacturers all trying to get you to try this and try that. It can make you lose your focus."

The words were coming from Dad's mouth, but they did not sound like him.

"Do you still want to get better?" he asked.

"Of course."

"I mean really better. Are you still really willing to do the things you need to do to improve your game?"

"Yes!" I was starting to feel a little defensive.

"Well, I'm wondering," he said.

"Wondering what?"

He paused for a long time.

"I'm wondering if I've taken you as far as you can go, as far as you can go with me."

Now this was getting strange. I had never heard my father express any sort of doubt about his capability as a teacher before.

"What are you taking about? Of course you haven't." I was starting to feel emotional. "It's my fault. You've never said, 'I can't give you the time.' I have to make more time. I have to put more into the lessons."

"I just wonder if there isn't somebody else who could take you to the next level," Dad said.

Now I was feeling nervous. I could not imagine my world without my father as my golf teacher.

"Dad, I could never work with somebody else. It's always been you and me. It wouldn't be fun if it was me and somebody else. We can go to Jack Lumpkin and talk about wedge play. We can talk to Peter Kostis about swing plane. We can talk to Paul Runyan about putting. We can go talk to that guy in South Carolina who taught us how to make sense of *The Golfing Machine.* We can talk to Hank Haney and Chuck Cook and Butch Harmon. But I need you to interpret for me what they all are saying."

For a while, we discussed these teachers, and some others, and what we might get from them. The odd thing, though, was that he never mentioned, not once, the one guy who really knew my swing well, the one guy my father loved almost like a third son: Jimmy Hodges. Jimmy worked with my father at Sea Island and at the golf schools. He was my father's protégé and my father was his mentor, and Jimmy was my closest friend even though he was 10 years older than me. Everything I knew about hunting and fishing I learned from Jimmy. If, in a different conversation on another day, I had asked my father, "Dad, if you couldn't teach me anymore, who would you want to teach me?" he would have said without a moment's hesitation, "Jimmy, of course." But the name of Jimmy Hodges never came up.

For a while, the conversation returned to its normal year-end tone, with my father saying let's do this and let's do that and I'll see you here and I'll see you there and we'll work with this guy and we'll work with that guy. We talked about goals for 1989, about winning tournaments, about improving in the majors, about making the Ryder Cup team, about putting away money, about Robin and Lexie and being a father and a husband and a breadwinner and the importance of finding fun in everything you do. I remember thinking, *This* is Dad. I know he wasn't just trying to shock me out of my stupor. That was not his style. I think he might have needed a little reassurance from me that I believed that he was and always would be the best teacher for me. Prior to that, it had never occurred to me that *his* confidence as a teacher could have been shaken by my dull play. To me, my mediocre play rested solely on my shoulders, but he saw it differently.

When I dropped him off at his house, he went inside to give me something he had never given me before: a copy of his book, *How to Feel a Real Golf Swing,* inscribed to me. As he left the truck he said, "Thanks for the good talk. Give a thought to what I said, though. Maybe there's a teacher out there who can do more for you now than I can, find the missing link." We shook hands. Dad waved. And then he was gone.

A week later, he was dead. Jimmy Hodges, sitting with him in the crowded cabin when the plane crashed into trees on a foggy night several miles from Jacksonville Airport, was dead, too. My life, as I knew it, was over.

FOLLOW YOUR DREAM

One of my father's favorite phrases was, "Follow your dream and enjoy the trip." It was hard for him to relate to people who didn't have dreams, for he was such a goal-oriented person. A lot of people my age are consumed by their desire for money and then don't know how to enjoy it if and when they get it. Others are made miserable by their quest for money. My father thought the accumulation of money was a poor goal. He thought winning the money title was a worthwhile goal not because it meant that you earned the most money, but because it meant you played the best over the course of the year. He encouraged me to think of each dollar as a point, like the points NASCAR drivers collect. The player with the most points deserves to be the envy of his peers. But regardless of where you finish on the money list, or in the pursuit of any other dream or goal, the critical thing is to enjoy the journey, the trip. Whenever he said that, and he said it often, I always assumed it was a sort of wink to me, since "Trip" was my nickname growing up, as it is for many people with III after their names.

CHAPTER 6

The Crash

I've thought often about the trip to Waycross I made with my father. Why did he say the things he said? Is it possible he knew that this would be our final conversation? (In the days between our trip and his death, we saw one another once briefly and chatted, but had no real conversation.) I believe that, in some way that cannot be articulated, he did know. My father was my teacher; I was his pupil. That was our relationship. If he could have known that any single conversation would be our last, his subject surely would have been teaching: who should teach me if he could not. He believed golf was never wholly knowable, that there is always more to learn, and that all golfers need teachers. From the age of 16, his teacher had been Harvey. From the time I was born, he was mine.

On the road home from Waycross, Dad prepared me, for the first time, for the idea that he would not always be there, that he could not always be there. My view of the world is not cosmic, but I do believe, as my father did, that everything happens for a reason; coincidence alone cannot explain why our last conversation was also our most dramatic, our most startling. Everything he wrote down on our Waycross trip—written on a fresh yellow legal pad—was in his briefcase in the plane and did not survive the crash. What survives is my memory of the conversation. It haunts me.

Robin and I were about to start a sort of working vacation. I had been invited to play in what is now my favorite postseason tournament, a friendly event with a generous purse called the Kapalua International in Maui, Hawaii. Lexie was six months old and Robin and I left her with my parents for the first time. This was going to be a break for Robin, and for me. Mark Rolfing, the tournament director, puts up the players in luxurious rooms, the weather is gorgeous, the course is fun, and there are a lot of festive dinners and parties. Mark had invited me to play in the tournament in 1986 and 1987 and I was very pleased to be invited back for 1988, particularly given how unspectacular my year had been.

The first night we were there, I ran into a pastor my parents knew from Atlanta, an old friend of my mother's, and we talked about having dinner together. Later that day I called home, just to check in, to see how Lexie was doing, but mostly to tell my mother about running into her friend. It was late afternoon for us, about 10 P.M. on the East Coast. My mom answered the phone. From her first word it was obvious that something was very, very wrong.

"I just got a call," she said, panicked. "They said Dad's plane has fallen off the radar. The fog is awful. There's no visibility."

Robin says the color drained from my skin the moment my mother came to the phone. I knew right then what had happened. I knew I'd never see my father again.

The details were slow to emerge. Dad and Jimmy Hodges and John Popa, the director of golf at Sea Island and a close friend of the family, were headed to Innisbrook, a golf resort near Tampa, for a couple of days of *Golf Digest* Instruction School meetings. They had a flight to an airport near the resort lined up from Jacksonville International Airport; to get from Sea Island to the Jacksonville airport they decided, as they often did, to charter a plane that could do the trip in about 20 minutes and at a nominal cost, rather than make a 90-minute drive. They had reserved a twin-engine plane, but a little single-engine plane, a Piper Cherokee, showed up instead. It was so small that it could not accommodate the three passengers and their golf bags; still, they decided to take it. The meetings, like the instruction schools, always started first thing in the morning, so you had to get in the night before, which is why they were flying off the day before. They decided to leave at about 8 P.M. so that Jimmy and John and my dad could have their dinners with their families before flying off.

As I talked to my mother, with the outcome of the flight still unknown, I knew I had to keep hope alive. "You know Dad," I told my mother. "He's probably talked the pilot into taking them all the way to Innisbrook." As I was saying these words, I knew it was not a rational thought. Planes don't just disappear off radars. You can't roam the air in a plane the way you can roam streets in a car. But I wanted to do anything I could to minimize my mother's worry before confirmation came.

I hung up the phone and went into a frenzy, telling Robin to pack everything. I made a flurry of calls trying to arrange flights off the island. I called my friend Jim Griggs in Monterey, California, to see if he knew how I could charter a jet to get us from California to Sea Island. Jim was not someone I knew particularly well then, but I knew he ran a big company and that he either had a corporate jet or had access to one. He said, "What time does your flight from Hawaii get into San Francisco?" I told him. He said, "When you land, a plane will be waiting to take you home." I was so grateful for his kindness, for his generosity. He said the exact words I needed to hear. All I wanted to do was get home as fast as I could. Jim was making it happen.

The plane ride from Hawaii to San Francisco was awful, not knowing if Dad was dead or alive. There was no way to get news while I was on the plane. It was six hours of the worst torture I could ever imagine, and it was just as bad for Robin. When we got off the plane Jim Griggs, whom I had met in a pro-am, was waiting for us. I said, "What are you doing here?" He had gotten up at 5:30 A.M. to get his plane from Monterey to San Francisco. "I'm here to take you home," he said. And I immediately thought of my father, how he always said you meet the most incredible people through golf, and how through golf you make a bond with people you might never make if you didn't share the game. In the years since the accident, Jim, who is about Dad's age, has become almost like a father to me.

I went to a pay telephone. Robin was sobbing, clinging to Jim's shoulder. She was a basket case, understandably; her love for my father was deep. We knew what was going to happen, but nothing can prepare you for the finality of it. Mark picked up the phone at home and I asked, "What did you find out?"

"They found the plane," he said. "There were no survivors."

Mark couldn't bring himself to say, "Dad is dead." He couldn't say, "Jimmy is dead." You lose *everything* at a moment like that, even language. He was going on reflex, I imagine, repeating the words the FAA officials had said to him, that all four men on the plane—my dad, Jimmy Hodges, their colleague John Popa, and the pilot, Chip Worthington—did not survive the crash.

My first reflexive thought was, "You should not be home alone now, Mark. I should be there with you and Mom." But the first words that came out were, "Mark, I'm so sorry," almost as if this whole nightmare were happening to somebody else and not to me. I felt guilt: for not being there, for Mark having to take care of Mom, for Mom talking on the phone while sitting on the floor, for Robin's uncontrollable sobbing, for my unresolved last conversation with Dad.

The details as to why the crash occurred were never fully resolved. The visibility that night was extremely poor. After reading all the reports, I feel that Dad's plane should have been warned away from even attempting to land. Through some combination of radar and radio miscommunication, Chip Worthington—who was an instrument-rated pilot, qualified to make an instrument-controlled landing—lost his position. He was attempting to fly his plane without sufficient help from controllers and without radar information that he should have had. The investigation into the accident indicated that Dad's plane got caught in the turbulence created by a commercial jet that had aborted a landing. I believe the pilot should have been told about the aborted landing by air traffic control; he was not. The plane crashed into a swamp several miles from the airport. The instrument readings indicate that he was not attempting to land at the time of the crash. A medical examiner told me later that the deaths of all four men must have been instantaneous. I don't imagine there was a moment the pilot turned around and said, "All right, men, prepare yourselves." I'd like to think that was the case. (My mother and Jimmy's wife and John's wife filed a lawsuit and won a significant out-of-court settlement. I wondered about the value of taking any legal action; my feeling was that once you start down that road you never get off it, not for the rest of your life. The money can't bring you satisfaction and the suit itself will only raise more questions than it will answer. The idea of having to answer questions, to have to make judgments about how much money a life is worth, about what you would accept in a settlement—to me that was just too horrible. My feeling was that Dad is dead. The only thing you can do is move on. I know that would have been his response. Mom thought differently. She was thinking not only of her needs, but her two grieving friends and their children as well.)

Chip Worthington, John Popa, Jimmy—they were all neighbors of ours, they all lived in or around St. Simons. The churches and the funeral homes were overwhelmed. St. Simons had never experienced such a tragedy, and everywhere you went the only thing people were talking about were the four deaths and who had seen whom last. In the days before Dad's funeral—the funerals of the three golf professionals were held on Wednesday, November 16, three days after the crash—I stayed at my mother's side as much as I possibly could. When possible, I went to see Susie Hodges, Jimmy's wife.

Even though Jimmy was 10 years older than me, we did everything together, and it had been that way since I was 18 and he was a 28-year-old assistant pro at Sea Island, working with and learning from my father, just as I was. Jimmy was a very good golfer and a long hitter, and all through high school and through much of college I knew that if I could beat Jimmy I was playing well. When he married Susie and started having kids—three in all, Nancy, Jason, and Wesley—I became only closer to him. I'd hang out with the kids and babysit for them, and I learned a lot about how to raise a family and how to act with children, which I never knew. Susie taught me how to change a diaper.

Jimmy was like a big brother to me. It was Jimmy who taught me how to hunt and fish, and those are two of the biggest passions in my life today. We'd hunt deer and ducks. We'd hunt with shotguns and bow and arrow. We'd surfcast and fly fish, from the shore and from boats. Jimmy knew all the inlets and coves and bays of St. Simons and Sea Island. He had permission from all the big land owners to go hunting, because they all knew him through golf and they all liked him. He had a magnetic personality; people were drawn to him. My father saw that in him. At the time of his death, at age 35, Jimmy was just starting to come into his own as a teacher, just starting to get instruction articles in the magazines, just starting to make a national name for himself as a teacher rooted in classical instruction. But at Sea Island, he was already beloved.

I remember the days before the funeral and right afterward as a

steady stream of sympathy visits, friends bring
food that nobody touched, meetings with lawyer
and FAA officials. The telephone would go hours
ringing, but the doorbell was ringing all the time an_ the letter carrier had stacks of mail. As I walked into the packed church for Dad's funeral, the only thing I could focus on was the coffin, made of some sort of metal, kind of an off-brown color, and the only thing I could think was, "This can't be happening, this cannot be happening." I don't know how I sat through the eulogies. I know they were well-intentioned, of course, but I could not sit there and listen to the words. I think the funeral started a period of hyperactivity for me that probably hasn't ceased since then. I found that I *had* to be doing something. When I did nothing, my mind could wander and that led to a state of depression. I'm doing it still. Robin says I've lost the ability to do nothing, and she's right. When we take the boat to the beach with friends, everybody else is laying out while I'm checking the engine or organizing tackle. I despise the word *relax.*

We all responded to Dad's death in different ways. In the weeks after the funeral, my mother would often say that she was going to take a shower and go to bed and I'd hear the water running and her sitting in the bathroom, sobbing. Other times we would all be together and then she'd suddenly say, "I'm going to walk the golf course," so she could grieve in private along the fairways where she and my father so often spent their afternoons.

I had a real fear of going back to tournament golf. I was petrified of the idea of going to an event and having everybody say to me, "So sorry to hear about your dad." I knew, of course, that the wishes would be heartfelt, and that I should be grateful for the concern of friends and even strangers. But I did not think I could handle what I knew would be a barrage of reminders about my father's death. I was just filled with dread. To get ready, I went to Sea Island's practice tee to hit balls. To be on that tee, on that very ground where Jimmy and Dad and I spent some of the happiest and most satisfying hours of my life—weeks, probably months, all added together—and to know that the three of us would never be gathered in that place again, it was nearly more than I could take. I never felt so alone in all my life.

The first tournament I went back to was the Chrysler Team Championship in early December, about three weeks after the accident. I played with Joey Sindelar, a good friend. Joey said, "It'll be good for you to play. We're going to have fun." But I was extremely nervous. I avoided eye contact with people. The first day there I was heading for the practice tee and the first person I saw was Andy Bean, who was heading somewhere in a golf cart. Andy is a gigantic, warm, gregarious man, a true son of the South, who for 10 seasons, from 1977 to 1986, was one of the best players in the game. We were friendly, but we didn't know each other well.

"Come on over here," he said. "Sit down, let's go for a ride." We started to go for a long ride in the cart and he started talking about his father and how his father taught him how to play, how golf was everything in his family growing up. He knew what I was going through. He said, "Your dad would want you to go out and play your best. That's all you can do. Go out, play your best and make him proud of you."

That gesture from Andy was important to me. For one thing, it broke the ice and broke it very effectively. It made me feel better. It eliminated a lot of my dread. And it made me realize that other people needed to respond to my father's death too, that they had things they wanted to say, for my benefit and for their own. For every tour player and tour official and writer and *Golf Digest* editor who passed along some kindness to me, and there were many, there were probably 10 strangers who did the same. They said things like, "Your dad gave me the best golf lesson I've ever had. I sure am going to miss him." One guy framed the notes my father had written for him after a lesson and gave the framed notes to me as a gift. I felt like saying to the man, "Hold on to these, they're going to help you a lot more than they're going to help me." But I realized that his true purpose was to make some sort of connection to my father through me. I had always known that my father was well-known in golf; what I didn't know was how well-liked he was. When I started to think about all these little encounters I had with people who knew my father, I realized that Dad made these people feel better about the future of their golf games, and for many people that meant feeling better about themselves. I think these people were convinced that my father had done things for them that no one else could do.

The frequency of these conversations has fallen with the passage of time, of course. People forget. I don't, my family doesn't; the accident is still horribly real, probably more real today than the day it happened. But I still hear from people who want to talk about my father more than occasionally. At the end of the 1996 season I was at Innisbrook, in Tarpon Springs, Florida, the place my father was trying to get to on the night he died. I was there playing with Beth Daniel, my regular partner for the JCPenney Classic, the annual mixed-team event. Beth was a student of my father's, a superb player and the better half of our team every year. We've won the event twice, in 1990 and 1995. Peter Kostis was at Innisbrook for the tournament. And Peter came up to me and said, "Davis, I'm sorry to burden you with this, but I have to tell you. I've just had one of the worst days I've had since your father's death. We taught a lot here together and we played a lot here, and the only thing I could think the whole day today was, 'This is where Davis made that really funny comment to that student,' or, 'This is where I holed out that chip to beat Davis and was he *fuming*.' I was missing him so much I couldn't keep it together." It was amazing to hear Peter say these words, because he's a confident, tough man, almost cocky. His tender side seldom comes out. But the memory of my father allowed a different side of Peter Kostis to emerge.

For a long while after my father's death, the guys who worked with my father and knew him—like Peter Kostis, Jack Lumpkin, Butch Harmon—were eager to help me with my swing, but I couldn't bring myself to accept their help. I was still clinging to my father. I tried a few lessons here and there, but every time a teacher expressed an idea, I heard with it a little voice in the back of my head saying, "What would Dad think of this change?" As a result, my game suffered.

I was fortunate to have a good relationship with Bob Rotella, the sports psychologist, before Dad died. Bob knew my father well. They respected each other; they were friends. My father asked Bob to write an afterword for his book. After the accident, Bob was someone I could talk to when I didn't know to whom to turn.

For many months after the accident I would wake up in the middle of the night and tears would be streaming down my face. My sobbing was uncontrollable. I wasn't dreaming that I was crying, I was actually crying. Other nights I would dream that Dad was going away on a business trip, or that I was going away to a golf tournament, and that we never returned from these trips or that when we did return we kept missing each other. I'd wake up in terror from these nightmares, screaming. It was horrible for Robin. It was horrible.

So I'd ask Bob about these dreams, about these crying fits. I'd say—and in this I reveal myself to be such a typical tour golfer it's embarrassing—what am I doing wrong? Bob would listen with incredible patience and explain that these are not issues with right answers and wrong answers. Then one day he said, "Look at what you're doing to yourself. You're trying to be the head of your family *and* your mother's family. You're trying to be a lawyer and an accountant for your father's estate. You're trying to play the tour.

You're trying to be your own swing coach. You're trying to put your father's death behind you. You're trying to prove to everybody that you can do everything, and the thing is you can't. Your mind and your body want to grieve, but you're not allowing the grieving to happen. Your father used to say when he was teaching you, 'I have a vote, Davis has a vote, and Davis's body has a vote.' Now you're violating your father's own rule. You're not listening to your body. Your body and mind want to grieve. Let them." That was a revelation. After that, I tried to let myself grieve. But I don't know if I ever did it effectively.

Not that I fully know what that means, to grieve effectively. People would say, "He's not dealing with it." Well, in one day, in one horrible moment, I lost my two best friends, my father and Jimmy Hodges. You go through that, and this will not be news to anybody who has endured anything similar, and you're scarred for life. You will never again be the person you were before the tragedy. Yes, you'll go to restaurants, tell stories, laugh at jokes, but deep down inside, in some place where only you can reach, you know that you are changed, that you've become a different person. Time heals and life goes on. But life's different now. What does it mean to handle tragedy well? I'll never know. My father was snatched away from me, with no warning, for no reason. Jimmy was, too. How are you supposed to react?

I played the 1989 season in a daze. Just about every tournament I went to, a local writer would want to know if I could talk about my father's death and its impact on me. I believe in being accommodating to the degree you can be, so I always said sure, but the effect these stories had on me, for good or for bad, was to keep the accident very fresh in my mind. All the while, my play was awful. I felt like I was slapping at the ball and I had no idea what to do to correct it. I finished the year 44th on the money list and didn't win a tournament. The first five months of the 1990 season weren't any better.

Then, in May of 1990, I was playing in a tournament in Japan. I had made the cut on the number; my play was dreadful. Jeff Sluman and Butch Harmon were watching me on the practice tee as I became more and more frustrated while hitting one poorly struck shot after another. They were silent. Finally, I turned to Butch and said, "What?"

"You really want to know?"

"Yes," I said, and I meant it.

And Butch basically read me the riot act. My grip was lousy, my weight transfer was wrong, my putting stroke was tentative, I wasn't giving my game the time it needed, and all I was doing on the course was frowning and ignoring the gallery. I wasn't listening to the people—he cited Jack Lumpkin specifically—who were in a position to really help me. Then he gave me a lesson, about weight transfer and shoulder turn, and for some reason I was ready to listen. I was like the alcoholic who can't really do anything about his drinking problem until he admits to himself he has a problem. That's where I was when I turned to Butch and said, "What?" It was an admission that I had bottomed out.

The benefit of putting my faith in Butch—really listening to what he was saying, really trying the moves he was suggesting—was instantaneous. On the weekend, I played very well and finished in a tie for third. Three months later, in August, I won my second tour event, The International, at Castle Pines in Colorado. And basically, I've been playing well since then (although my play in 1994 was dull without being horrendous; I didn't win a tournament and finished 33rd on the money list). In 1991, I won at Hilton Head for the second time. In 1992, I won three events in five weeks. In late March, I won the Players Championship, in Ponte Vedra, 15 miles from where my father's plane crashed. Two weeks later I won at Hilton Head, my third win there, and then the following week I won at Greensboro. In 1993, I won the Tournament of Champions and the Las Vegas Invitational. I was also on the Ryder Cup team, and the next year I was on the inaugural Presidents Cup team. In 1995, I won in New Orleans and finished second the following week at the Masters, and was again on the Ryder Cup team. Fred Couples and I won the World Cup in 1992, 1993, 1994, and 1995. In 1996, I won in San Diego, finished in a tie for second at the U.S. Open and played on the second Presidents Cup team. I'm writing this before the start of the 1997 season. I'm 32. I feel like I'm ready to bust loose.

Something happened that day on a practice tee in Japan with Butch Harmon. I let something go. Not all of it, but something. Then, at The International, I let some more go—not all of it, but some more. I said to myself, "You've been dragging around a lot of stuff for a long time. You're taking all the fun out of the game. You keep trying to prove something to yourself, and the only thing you need to prove is that the game is still fun." All I could think after Dad died was, "Golf will go on, but it will never be fun again." When I was home, I never played golf with my friends; I would play tournament golf or no golf at all. Then, at The International, golf suddenly was fun again. I came home afterward and had some casual games with friends, and *that* was fun. I finished a shot out of a playoff at the 1995 Masters, and *that* was fun, being in the hunt was fun. Even the 1996 U.S. Open, when I made bogeys on the last two holes and finished a shot out of first, *that,* in its own torturous way, was fun. Smarted like hell to not win, sure, but it was fun to be in the thick of it. I was fulfilling my father's credo. I was letting golf be fun again. I was playing with joy. I know I don't often show it on the outside, but I know what I feel on the inside, and I feel my sense of joy from the game in a deep and significant way. I haven't let it all go yet. I know I never will. My father was taken from me long before his time. He was taken from my brother, my mother, my wife, my daughter, and from the son I named for him whom he'll never meet, not on this earth. There will always be pain.

At tournaments, people sometimes ask me if I think about my father coming down the stretch with a title on the line. The answer is yes, I think about my father in those situations. I think about my father when I'm playing on Father's Day in the U.S. Open, when I'm playing at home with friends, when I'm hitting pitch shots in the backyard with my children. When I put my tee in the ground, he's there. When I pull my ball out of the hole, whether I've made a birdie or a par or a bogey, he's there. On every drive and every chip and every putt, he's there, somewhere.

LETTERS

After my father died, our family received hundreds of letters from well-wishers, from politicians, from famous golfers, from successful businessmen, from kids, from caddies, from people from every walk of life. Here is one from Barbara Nicklaus, addressed to my mother.

Dear Penta,

We just wanted you to know how shocked and sorry we were about Davis, and to let you know that we'll be thinking of you.

He touched so many lives in such a wonderful way, and he certainly will be missed.

Our love and prayers are with you in the difficult days ahead.

With love and sincere sympathy,
Jack and Barbara Nicklaus and family

This was a letter my mother received from a teenage boy who lived on Sea Island named Kipp Bankston, whom my father helped with his golf swing as a favor, because he saw how much the boy liked the game.

Dear Mrs. Love,

I was deeply hurt by the tragic death of your husband. Mr. Love and yourself have always been especially kind to Mike and I. I have and always will feel that Mr. Love was a very extraordinary man. I believe he has earned the respect and love of everyone who knew him.

Love,
Kipp

This letter was from Pete Davison, who was an assistant to my father at the Atlanta Country Club. Pete today runs the entire TPC golf club network for the PGA Tour.

Dear Penta,

I know this has been an extremely difficult time for you and the boys. However, I hope there has been some solace in the outpouring of affection that everyone has shown for Davis and your family.

I wanted you to know that Davis has had the biggest influence on my life professionally of all of the people I have known in the golf business. He helped teach me the business and the standards and values that go along with being a golf professional. For years, every time I was faced with a problem I would ask myself, "How would Davis handle this?"

There is no one that I had more respect and admiration for than Davis Love, Jr. I will miss him tremendously.

I want to offer my help with anything that you may need and, in particular, that Mark or young Davis may need. If Mark ever needs advice or help in golf, the golf business, school, or any related way, please allow me to help shape his future. You know I think the world of Davis III and would be happy to offer my services anytime he needs someone to talk to or someone to help him.

We all love you and the boys and suffer with you in this time of grief.

Warmest regards,
Pete Davison

This letter, again to my mother, was from Mr. Penick, written by hand and with great care, both in his antique penmanship and in the words he selected.

Dear Penta:

It was such a shock when we were called about Davis. He was one of my favorites. Helen joins me in our prayers. He will probably be teaching in Heaven.

I have not only had back problems, but I have shingles; my excuse for the poor handwriting.

Now, if I can ever help with either of the boys, please call on me.

Our deepest sympathy,
Helen and Harvey Penick

CHAPTER 7

Robin

It would be hard to imagine two people more different than my wife, Robin, and my father. For one thing, when we first started going out, Robin knew nothing about golf, and my father's whole life was golf. But over the years they became very close. I think my father helped Robin understand what it means to lead a golfing life, and I think Robin taught my father that it's possible to lead a fulfilled life without golf. What they shared in common was . . . well, it's probably better to let Robin tell you herself about my father, me, and our relationship.

ROBIN:

I am not a golfer, and I don't necessarily think of myself as a golfer's wife, although I realize that when I go to tournaments and people see me that's *all* they think I am. People will say, "Hey, that's Davis Love's wife." In that setting, I don't have a name and I really don't need one. When Davis is at a tournament, I *am* Davis's wife. But the rest of the time, I don't think of myself as being married to a well-known golfer. I think I'm married to a guy named Davis who happens to make his living playing golf. It's important for the wife of a tour player to have her own identity. I run the house, get our two children to school and to their friends' houses, to their tennis lessons, to the doctor's office when they're sick. I cook, I exercise, I go out with my friends. I lead a life. On the tour, I'm Davis's wife.

Davis's father prepared me for that. He prepared me for a lot of things. When I hear about how Davis grew up, it was like *Ozzie and Harriet,* like a TV show. Everything was so well-ordered. When I'd go to Davis's parents' house when Davis and I were courting, and all they'd be talking about was golf, I couldn't believe it. I felt like saying, "I don't know anything about golf. Can we please talk about something else?" But I never did. Instead I listened as if I knew who Jack Nicklaus was and what a flying right elbow was all about. To be perfectly truthful, I'm still a little fuzzy on what a flying right elbow is. I do know that what I did come to appreciate is that golf is a game of order, and that golf provided an incredible amount of order in the Love house, and a lot of stability, and a lot of sharing.

Golf can be so overwhelming! The amount of time Davis and his dad spent together, I certainly never spent time like that with my father. Davis's father would go to all these tournaments, record every shot Davis took, go over them all after the round, day after day and week after week and month after month. If he couldn't be at a tournament, then they would talk on the telephone every day, hole by hole, shot by shot. For hours. When we were first married, I said to myself, "No, this can't be. It's not really going to be like this." But I got used to it. When they were getting into one of their conversations, I'd just go for a walk. Then it got to be that I liked it, even though I couldn't contribute to the conversations. I learned that my father-in-law's whole life was his two sons. He taught Davis to be a player. He taught Mark, who was probably more naturally talented than Davis but not as devoted, to be a teacher; that's why Mark is so effective as Davis's caddie. Golf was his way of connecting himself to his sons.

Davis and I were best friends in high school, but we never went out together. Then when we did start going out, when Davis was home from college in the summer, I immediately started spending a lot of time with his family, which was weird for me, because I'd never spent that much time with a family before. By the Loves's standards, I was a little wild then: I went out to dinner a lot, went to bars, listened to bands, hung out with my friends, slept late, had a good time. Davis's dad and I were very different, but he was so nice to me from the beginning. I think he realized early on that Davis and I were in love, and that if he didn't embrace me he was going to lose a son. That takes a lot of wisdom, but that's the kind of man he was. He was wise.

When I became pregnant with Lexie, Davis and I had been married for just eight months and it just about killed me. We were going to see the world, do all these things, have all this fun. And then I go and get pregnant. I went to see Davis's parents. I was crying. And Davis's father said to me, "We know you're upset. But you have to understand that everything happens for a reason and everything's going to work out fine. Penta and I are very excited that you're pregnant and that you're going to have our first grandchild. We're not young and we're certainly not going to become young now, and we're just so happy that we're going to have a grandchild before we get too old to enjoy the baby. And we're going to take that baby whenever you need us to, and you're going to be able to travel and do all the things you want to do. This is not the end of things. It's the beginning."

And he was absolutely correct. When Lexie came, he and Penta were so filled with joy and were such wonderful grandparents. And then Davis Jr. died six months after Lexie was born. I'm just so glad Davis and I could give him six months with that baby before he died, because he loved her so. He made me realize that everything does happen for a reason. Lexie and her brother Dru are the joys of our life.

When I think of my years with Davis, there are really two periods: before my father-in-law's death and afterward. We were in Hawaii for a tournament when his plane crashed. Davis had just run into a man, a preacher at a church where Davis's mom worked when Davis was a boy in Atlanta, and we were talking about having dinner with him, and Davis was just so thrilled with running into this guy he wanted to call home and tell his mother. I had just taken a shower and was getting dressed and I heard Davis say, "Mom, this is ridiculous. Just go ahead and tell me. I can tell something's wrong." And then I heard him say, "We'll take the next plane back." So Davis hangs up and I say, "We're not going back anywhere. Your parents can deal with whatever it is." I figured it was an ear infection with Lexie or something. And then I looked at Davis and he was absolutely white, all the color was drained from his face. He just said, "My dad's plane has disappeared on the radar." I felt sick.

We flew out of Hawaii and we were in the airport in San Francisco, on a pay phone by the baggage claim. I could still point out the exact phone. I was pacing behind Davis and I heard him say, in a really calm voice, "You're absolutely positive—there were no survivors?" He was talking to Mark. He was so calm. And from that moment on, Davis took control. He took charge. I believe in some basic ways he became his father.

Davis is the same kind of father his father was. The exact same. And I wouldn't want it any other way. Davis talks with our oldest child—our daughter, Lexie—as if she were an adult. He'll reason everything out with her. I'll say to Davis, "You're talking to a seven-year-old girl as if you were talking to me and you think she understands everything, and I'm telling you I don't know that she does." And Davis will say, "My dad talked to me this way and I understood, and I'll talk to her this way and she'll understand, too."

People sometimes say to me, "Has Davis come to terms with his father's death?" The only way I know to answer is to say Davis *became* his father on the day his father died. Which is to say he's a different person than he was before. I think now he's trying to prove himself to himself. Before, I think he was trying to prove himself to his father. When his dad was alive, he was, sometimes anyway, miserable because his dad was making him practice all the time. He wasn't going out on his Harley, or going out on a boat, going fishing or hunting. Because he was practicing. Because his father was demanding. He wasn't hard on the boys, but he demanded excellence. If you think it's possible to become a world-class *anything* without someone making demands on you, I think that's naive. Now when he practices, he's doing it for himself. Before his death, Davis was always saying, "My dad's going to show me the right way, my dad's going to help me win a tournament, my dad's going to tell me what I need to do." Then one day he didn't have his dad anymore and he had to figure things out for himself, and he did.

I think it's really hard for Davis to talk about his father. It's hard for any child to lose a parent, under any circumstance. But when your father is young, and he's your coach, and your best friend too, that's more than any one person can stand, really. He'll talk about things his father did in the past, but he can't say, "If my father were here today he'd say—whatever." One night after his father died, Davis just broke down and cried and cried and cried. One night. Davis's dad traveled a lot, and I sometimes think Davis still imagines that his father is on one of his long trips that he just hasn't returned from yet.

It's not easy being a parent. I'm sure it's not easy being a father.

Davis's dad was the most tolerant man in the world, he paid no attention to race or religion or wealth; he lived by the credo do unto others as you would have them do unto you. The only time he was intolerant was when it came to his two sons. If Davis wasn't practicing enough, his father would let him have it. When Davis and Mark were in college, they did the stupid things college kids do; when they came home too late, having drunk too much, Davis's father was even-voiced but really clear: If you're going to live under this roof, you're not going to behave like that. Mark and Davis might have had a period of recklessness, but it was shorter than it was for most people, and never out of control. The brothers had too much respect for their father, who taught them to look out for each other, which they do. Mark knows that Davis would do anything for him, and Mark would do anything for Davis. That's why they're such a good team, on the course and off. That's how their father raised them.

There's always been a lot of talk about Davis winning majors and why hasn't he won majors, and if his dad were still alive, would he have won majors by now? I don't know. It's really hard to say what happens on a subconscious level. I know he should have won a couple of majors by now, and I don't know why he hasn't. He could have won the 1995 Masters, but Ben Crenshaw, in the wake of Harvey Penick's death, seemed destined to win that one, and Davis came up a stroke short. He could have won the 1996 U.S. Open. It does sometimes seem like Davis does not have good luck, and it does take some luck to win a major. I know it will be a very emotional moment for him when he does win a major, because it's a goal for him, and because his father was such a goal-oriented person. Maybe that will open a floodgate for Davis, make him think of his father in a new way, let him think of his father in the present tense for a change. Like, "If Dad were here now, he'd be so happy!" The only references he makes to his father now are in the past tense.

But part of me thinks that this whole thing about the majors is overstated, too. The thing that Davis's dad always emphasized with me is that golf is supposed to be fun. The majors never seem like much fun. The tournaments in Hawaii, they're fun. When my father-in-law gave me lessons, the only thing he emphasized was having fun. All those rules and everything, he knew it was pointless to teach them to me, because he knew I didn't care about them. I'd play a few holes with him, hit my ball into a trap or whatever you're supposed to call that thing, and then I'd throw the ball out, because I surely didn't have the golf skill necessary to get it out with a club. And Davis's dad would just laugh. He knew there was more than one way to play the game. Now of course he wouldn't want me out there when there was serious golf going on, or a serious lesson. But he wanted me to have fun. He knew I was more interested in putting than in other parts of the game, so that's what he emphasized. He'd say, "Follow through to the hole." I always thought that was so sweet of him, to take an interest in my pathetic golf game. Of course, he had this fantasy, I suppose, that I would develop a real interest in golf the way his wife did, and that golf would be something that Davis and I would be able to do together. Well, we *do* do golf together: He plays, and I watch.

I think the biggest win in Davis's career so far must be The Players Championship, which he won in 1992. They always say the Players Championship is the most demanding field of the year, a better field than even the U.S. Open, and the course, the Stadium course in Ponte Vedra, leaves no room for error, because there's water on 18 holes, or at least it seems that way. You probably know the 17th hole, the par-3 with the island green. Either you knock the ball on the green or you're fishing in your bag for another ball.

Anyway, the course is just a few miles from where Davis's father's plane went down, and I don't think there's any way not to be aware of that when you're there. I know there isn't for me and I suspect the same is true for Davis. On the Sunday of the '92 tournament, the weather was nasty: cold and gray, clouds all over. And then, just as Davis was finishing up on the 18th green and winning the tournament, the skies cleared. First the sun just sort of peeked through, and in no time it was a bright sunny day. And the next thing we knew we were all on the 18th green, Davis and his mom and Lexie and me—our son wasn't born yet—and the sky was just so dramatic because it had changed so quickly from a gloomy, dark day. And I said to Davis, "That's your dad, shining down at you in your moment of glory. And he's saying, 'I'm watching you, I'm proud of you, I'm still here to guide you, and I love you.'"

CHAPTER 8

Brotherly Love

Every year my brother Mark has caddied for me full time I've had a banner year. He was on the bag in 1992, 1995, and 1996, and in each of those years I surpassed $1 million in earnings on the tour. Being a tour caddie is a tough business. The hours are long, you're on the road and away from your family a lot, and there can be a fair bit of anxiety, since your income is dependent on what your player is making. Mark handles all of that incredibly well. But beyond all that, there are so many little ways Mark helps me, on the course and off the course. If you ask most touring pros what they're looking for in a caddie, they'll say they want somebody who knows when to talk, what to say when it's time to talk, and when to say nothing. Mark does that better than any caddie I've ever had. Of course, he's had the most practice. We've known each other since June 30, 1966, the day Mark was born, two years, two months, and 17 days after I arrived.

MARK:

I realize that in a lot of ways I'm not a typical tour caddie. For one thing, I have regular work with one of the best players in the game, and I did from the day I became a tour caddie. I didn't have to come up through the ranks, unless you count the 20 or so years Davis and I lived under the same roof as coming up through the ranks. For another thing, I don't typically have a roommate, unless I'm rooming with Davis, which I might do a half-dozen or so times a year. For another thing, I'm sometimes able to hitch a ride with my boss to the next tour stop on the corporate jet he leases. I know I have it good.

Still, I want to be accepted by the other tour caddies; I don't want to distance myself from them. When my caddie badge can't get me into clubhouses—and it only can on Tuesdays, when I'm lugging Davis's golf bag in its travel case, getting ready for a new week—I could easily produce my player's family badge to gain access. But I don't. Instead, I get mad.

Whenever I see a sign that says "Professionals Only, Caddies Not Permitted," I really resent it. I guess it bothers me because it's such a powerful reminder that to be a caddie is to be subservient, and that's just not the way Davis and I operate. Of course, the player is the boss and the caddie is the employee, but any good player-caddie relationship has the feel of a partnership. I know many of the old-timers, my father's generation and the generation before that one, have a hard time with even the concept of a real caddie-player partnership; in the old days, if there was a relationship between the caddie and the player, the caddie's job was to provide comic relief. The caddie was sometimes, although certainly not always, a character who told stories about bar brawls and scrapes with the law and kept his player loose. All that's changed. If you caddie for a top-30 player you are likely to be making at least $80,000 a year, and very possibly twice that. It's a profession. On the European tour, where the money is nothing like it is in the United States, they already understand that. It's different here. At every tournament, I'll have people yell at me, "Hey, caddie, how far was that shot?" I suppose those are the same people who go to a restaurant and say, "Hey, waiter, I dropped my spoon, go get me another one." Davis thinks most of the rules for caddies are silly. He'll say, "Take that bib off, it's 98 degrees." Still, I won't take it off unless he says so. He's the boss.

I often wonder what my dad would think of my working for Davis as his caddie. The times he did see me caddie for Davis, like at the tour qualifying school, he was pleased. He thought I was good for Davis's game. On the other hand, he was very intent on my carving out my own niche for myself, and now my identity is plainly entwined with Davis's. At the time of my father's death I was 21, just about to start the last semester of my senior year of college at Valdosta State, where I played on the golf team. He and I were talking often about my becoming a teacher, a teaching pro, and our working at Sea Island together. My mother would say things to my father like, "OK, you've got Davis all in one piece. He's married. Robin and Davis have a baby. He's won his first tour event. He's fine. Now you've got to work on Mark." The natural thing for us to consider was teaching. I guess I had a little thought of maybe still trying to play professionally, but my game wasn't making the kinds of strides it needed to consider tournament golf really seriously. If I was to be really honest, through my first two years of college—when I was at the University of North Carolina, the same school Davis attended—I had a hard time being very serious about *anything.*

At one point, when I was still at North Carolina, Dad gave me a bunch of golf instruction books to read and said, "You need to know the swing." And I said, "I think I know the swing." He got hot at me for that. He had dedicated his life to figuring out the golf swing and he knew he didn't know everything there was to know about it. So who was I to be talking in this arrogant way? But I was a kid, and kids think they know everything. It's only when you get older that you realize how little you know. I'm glad my father made me read those books. There's a lot of wisdom in the classic golf books, and reading them teaches you how much there is to know.

I suppose I'm still looking for my career, but whatever it is I know it will be in golf. Being Davis's caddie is not my career, even though I like it a great deal. If the course design business Davis and I are involved in takes off, I could see that as a career. I could still imagine teaching. The one career I know I won't have is as a touring pro. I've known that from the day Dad died. After the crash, we had Christmas break, then I went back to Valdosta for the last semester of my senior year. In the fall I had been playing well, and I thought about attempting tournament golf. The spring after my father died I played in one college tournament. My play was awful. My heart wasn't in it. I haven't played any serious competitive golf since then.

The most significant difference between Davis and me is that practice makes him better and it makes me worse. It's hard for a teacher like my father, or any golf instructor, to accept that some players don't get much, if anything, out of practice, and it's taken me a long time to accept that. But I know for me it's true. When I tried to get better I got worse. Someone who is really interested in details is likely to be a very good practicer. That's Davis. When he goes fishing, he has to know every aspect of what he's doing: How to fix the engine. How to rig the lures. What the chop on the water should be like to catch fish. Someone who is just interested in the big picture is maybe not as likely to be a good practicer. That's me. I might enjoy fishing as much as Davis, but I'm not interested in the details; just put a rod in my hands and I'm very happy. I'm playing the best golf I've ever played now. I probably break par one in four rounds and I'm seldom more than three or four over par, from the back tees, and I never practice, except hitting balls for 15 minutes to warm up before a round. If my game keeps improving, I harbor a dream about playing in national amateur golf events in the future. The ultimate dream for me—and my game has miles to go if this is ever going to happen—would be to play for the United States on the Walker Cup team in 2001. That's the year the Walker Cup will be played at Ocean Forest, the wonderful new Rees Jones course on Sea Island where Davis, Mom, and I are all members.

If I do make it, I'd bet I'd be the first player in Walker Cup history to look at the hole while putting, regardless of how long or how short the putt is. I know it looks odd, but it just makes sense to me. My father used to say if you want to throw a ball into somebody's outstretched hand, you don't look at the ball, you look at the outstretched hand. Well, I've applied that same principle to putting.

I think one of the reasons Davis likes having me on the bag is that I'm an unspoken but constant reminder of Dad. For instance, Dad thought hitting balls after a round was very important, so you can fine tune what you've just done on the course. Most tour golfers go to the practice tee after a round, but most go just as a force of habit. Davis will go and he'll see Mike Hulbert over here and Freddy Couples over there, and he has me set up the bag in a place where he knows he can get some good conversation in. It's understandable, because after a round you have a lot of pent-up things that you'd like to get off your chest to a good friend. But as my father would say, "Don't fool yourself into thinking that that's practicing." When Davis is shooting the breeze instead of really concentrating on the pile of balls in front of him, all he has to do is glance at me and he knows what I'm thinking. I'll glance over at Greg Norman or Nick Faldo. Those guys never get distracted. Davis gets the message without a word being said. He's hearing my father say, "Don't fool yourself."

As I write this, at the end of the 1996 season, Davis is sometimes described as the best player never to have won a major. That's not a tag he wants, but it's one that a lot of good players have had over the years until they shed it, like Tom Kite did in 1992 and Corey Pavin did in 1995. Maybe if Dad had never died he would have won majors by now—who knows? I know it's an important goal for him. I think it's taken Davis a long time to realize that you don't have to play flawless golf for 72 holes to win a major. This may sound egotistical, but it's true: Davis doesn't have to play his best to beat an entire field. That's what he learned at the 1995 Masters, when he finished a shot behind Ben Crenshaw, and that's what he learned at the 1996 U.S. Open, when he finished a shot behind Steve Jones. I feel that it's only been since Davis turned 30 that he's even had the necessary experience to win majors. Now he knows how to win them.

After the accident, it seemed to me that I had to be the one of the three of us who was least affected by Dad's death. I put on a face for people that said, Everything's going to be OK, even though I didn't necessarily believe it. I did it because for a while there Mom and Davis couldn't do that, and in some ways they still can't. When Lynn and I had our first baby late in 1996, Mom was overjoyed, of course, but then she got very sad, because she was thinking about how much Dad would have loved to see the baby. Davis is the same way. It's very difficult for him to talk about Dad without becoming very emotional.

I think I've come to terms with Dad's death in the sense that I recognize that I got from my father all that I'm going to get. The interaction is over. The relationship is not going to evolve. I can think about my relationship with my father with contentedness. I don't think my mother is there yet and I'm not sure if Davis is, either. It's possible that that has held Davis back. The influence of the mind is such a hard thing to understand in golf. Davis had so much admiration and respect and dependency on Dad it might be hard for him to say, I can win a U.S. Open or a Masters or a British Open without you being right here. But I think as he's getting older he's getting over that. Davis is 32 years old as I write this. The next decade is his chance to make the kind of mark on the game he expects to make. When Davis and I were kids, we always wanted to show Dad how good he were. Davis still does. I do, too. Each in our own way.

CHAPTER 9

Penta Love

My mother, Penta Burgin Love—she was the fifth girl in her family; there were 13 children in all—is a very good golfer. I played with my mom a lot when I was a kid, and for years she was the person I was trying to beat. I don't think I did beat her until high school.

As kids, Mark and I would look in the paper at the LPGA scores and see a lot of the women shooting 74 and 75. We'd say, "Hey, Mom, you can make those scores. Why don't you go out on tour and make some money?" She was probably 40 or so at the time. And she'd say, "If I went on the ladies' tour, who would take you to hockey practice, who would prepare Dad's dinner? Who would make sure your homework was done?" Our point exactly.

Mom was always impressed by stories of how her mother-in-law drove my father around Arkansas and Texas, even all the way to Colorado, to take my father to junior golf tournaments when he was a boy. And that was in the days when going a hundred miles in a car could be an all-day adventure. Mom followed her mother-in-law's example superbly.

Mom is also an excellent teacher. She'll say things like, "I don't know what you're doing, but you're not concentrating like you were last week." Sometimes she'll say technical things. Her favorite thing to say, in regard to my putting, is, "Davis, you're reading too much break." I'll say, "You know, Mom, these greens on tour are a little faster than what we've got at home." She is never moved. "Too much break, Davis, too much break," she'll say. My putting problems are her specialty. She'll say, "You've got the toe of your putter up in the air again." Or, "Your head's coming up." She knows what she's talking about. She learned from the best.

PENTA:

There were two men named Davis in my life: my husband, Davis Milton Love, Jr., and my first son, whom we named for his father and his father's father, and whom we called Trip. They shared a name, and an incredible passion for golf. They were best friends, but they were very different people. Davis Jr. had to plan out everything, write down everything, while Davis III has always been willing to figure things out as he goes along. I have filing cabinets filled with Davis's notes, hundreds and hundreds of pages. I'm not sure anybody can make heads or tails of them, except for Davis III and Mark. Every time Davis went to work in seminars with other teachers, he'd write down thoughts about the game he had heard from other teachers and start a new file. Bob Toski. Peter Kostis. Jack Lumpkin. Claude Harmon. Paul Runyan. They all had files. The only teacher he didn't have a file for was Harvey Penick. What Harvey taught, that was all in Davis's head. Davis passed on a lot of Harvey to both the boys. Harvey was like a father to Davis.

Davis was first introduced to golf by his father, while growing up in El Dorado, Arkansas. Davis caddied for his dad and became infatuated with the game. Golf was not a family game for the Loves; Davis's father was the only golfer in the family. The rest of his family was involved in politics, religion, and farming, mostly in Mississippi. They were Southern aristocrats. My husband's paternal grandfather, Mark Perrin Lowrey Love, was an acting lieutenant governor of Mississippi in the 1920s and spent 20 years in the Mississippi State Senate. He was the first layman to be elected vice president of the Southern Baptist Convention. Davis Jr. stood in awe of his paternal grandfather's accomplishments and we named our second son after him.

Davis Jr.'s father wanted a different life. He migrated west to Arkansas and Texas to try to make money in oil. He was a geological engineer and a brilliant man with a strong entrepreneurial instinct. He'd go from Colorado to Paris to Saudi Arabia, for long periods at a time, to pursue his business interests. He made large sums, but it wasn't easy for him to hold on to it, because he was often investing his own money in his next project and you could never know which project was going to succeed and which would fail. I think that his father's experiences taught Davis Jr. to be very careful, very conservative, with his money. I don't know how much of that rubbed off on my son Davis. He puts his money away, but he's not afraid to spend it.

Davis Jr. left home for the University of Texas when he was 17. That's where he met Harvey; Harvey was the head professional at the Austin Country Club and the golf coach of the University of Texas team. Davis had many scholarship offers, but he chose Texas because of Harvey's reputation. Davis was an only child and was always younger than his classmates, so socially he was probably a bit awkward; that's why golf was such a good fit for him. It was something he could do on his own. Harvey saw right away how much Davis loved the game and how intent he was on improving. Harvey had a warmth about him and a level of integrity I've never known in anybody else. He had real character. Davis idolized him.

I remember shortly after we were married, when Davis was working as the professional at the Charlotte Country Club, Harvey came to Charlotte for a teaching seminar and he came to our house for breakfast. Davis was just so excited to have the opportunity to cook breakfast for this man. That was one of the highlights of his life; that's how much Harvey meant to him. Years later, when we were at the Atlanta Country Club, Harvey came and stayed with us for three days. For Davis, that was just about like going to heaven. My son Davis never got to know Mr. Penick that well but he always felt close to him because of his father. Davis III treasures the time he spent with Harvey. I'm pleased that Davis understands that an appreciation for golf is something to be handed down, generation to generation.

My husband was careful about not pushing golf on Davis and Mark. He had seen other parents push golf on their children, and that generally turns kids off from the sport. Davis made sure the kids had access to balls and clubs, but he never gave instruction of any kind unless they asked. When they did ask, Davis was very careful to give them just enough to motivate them to want them to play more. Once Mark said to his father, "Dad, I can't get the ball in the air." Mark was five and he was trying to hit drivers off the ground and he was hitting nothing but ground balls. Davis went to the pro shop, got out a 5-wood, cut the shaft in half, put a grip on it and said, "Try this." Mark went out with it and started getting the ball in the air right away. I've got that 5-wood in a closet, waiting for Dru and Lexie, if they ever want it.

Davis Jr. knew that the best discoveries are the ones a student makes for himself. Other teachers would say to Davis, "Your boy's got a funny looking grip." And Davis would say, "That's OK. You leave him alone. As long as he's having fun." Davis III was holding the club cross-handed for awhile, and Davis never said a thing. Then one day Davis came to his dad and said, "How come everybody else holds the club different than I do?" So that's when Davis got his first lesson on the grip, at about age seven. It continued that way for a long while, very informally. Davis would go out and play a few holes or hit a few balls, then move on to some other activity. He was just goofing around.

Then, when Davis was ten, he and his father, who was playing in the tournament, went to the 1974 PGA Championship at Tanglewood in Winston-Salem, North Carolina. When Davis III came home from that, he said, "Some day, I'm going to play in that tournament." He saw Arnold Palmer in the lockerroom. He ate breakfast with Sam Snead. He saw Jack Nicklaus on the practice tee. He saw that his father knew these golfing celebrities and that these people respected his father. I think that's when he first got bit by the golf bug, and when he first started seeing his father as someone extraordinary. Davis became far more keen to play after that.

Then, when Davis was 13, things changed. We had moved to Sea Island so that Davis Jr. could become a full-time golf teacher. One day Davis III suddenly said to his father, "Dad, I want to get really good at golf." And his father said, "How hard are you willing to practice?" And Davis said, "I'll do whatever you think is necessary." To which Davis Jr. said, "If you are, then I'll do whatever it takes to help you reach your goals. But you've got to be willing to listen to me." Davis Jr. never had to say those words to Davis again. My husband could see right away that his son had an incredible desire to be the best he could be.

Once we made the move away from the Atlanta Country Club and to Sea Island, Davis's traveling schedule for the *Golf Digest* Instruction Schools was grueling. Some years he'd be away as much as 30 weeks. He didn't feel guilty about being away so much—he was making a living for his family and doing the thing he loved to do. But he felt a loss, the loss of not being with his children night after night. So when he was home, he did everything in his power to spend as much time as possible with the boys. Davis never booked lessons after 4 P.M. on school days, because that was when he and Davis and Mark could play together or go to the practice tee if that's what the boys felt like doing. Other days, the boys wanted to go fishing and crabbing, and Davis Jr. would join them in that, too. Sometimes, after fishing, they'd hit balls through dusk and into the night.

After that conversation in which Davis told his dad he wanted to get really good, Davis began devoting his summers to golf. He'd wake up and go to the practice tee. He'd play 18 holes, or 27 holes, or 36 holes, in the afternoon. Then he'd return to the practice tee to hit balls and do drills with his father. Davis's golf was improving all the time.

Still, his father wondered if the lessons were sinking in. Davis Jr. would come home from practice sessions with Davis and say, "I don't think he heard a word I said today." And then a week later Davis might say, "Remember, Dad, last Tuesday when we were talking about the position at the top? Is it bad to go past parallel?" He'd make a swing in front of a mirror. "Is this what you had in mind?" My husband would be amazed. He'd say, "Just when you think he doesn't hear anything, you realize that he hears *everything.* And he remembers it, too."

When Davis Jr. died, I worried more for Mark than for Davis. Davis was already set in his profession and he had so much technical skill. I knew he'd have the desire to keep improving. Shortly before the accident, Davis said to me that he had taken Davis III about as far as he could with the technical aspects of the swing, that all he'd need to continue to get better was superior coaching. He also said, "I've got a lot more to do for Mark." Mark had many interests outside golf and had not devoted the time to golf that Davis had. Mark was talking to his father about going into teaching. Davis Jr. had a dream about building a golf learning center at Sea Island; he was thinking that if Mark decided not to pursue tournament golf, the golf learning center at Sea Island would be a great teaching base for Mark, and for himself. Davis was every bit as devoted to Mark as he was to Davis III. When somebody would say to Davis, "How's your son?" he'd say, "Which one?" Davis wanted Mark to know about his golf files, what was in them, how they were organized, how to read them.

Davis had files for everything—for golf, for personal subjects, for business matters. He was talking to me about all his many files one night and he said, "If anything ever happens to me, you'll know where all the good stuff is." And I thought to myself, "What do you mean, if anything ever happens to you? What in the world would I do if anything ever happened to you?" I distinctly remember saying to myself, "I'm not even going to think about that possibility."

A few days after that conversation we had our 26th wedding anniversary. And he gave me a ring, a beautiful diamond anniversary ring. He was funny about gifts. He loved art and antiques and he was always taking me to art galleries and antique stores, looking to buy things spur of the moment. He loved impressionist paintings and American primitive and French country antiques. Then, come Christmas, I might get a box of golf balls. But anniversaries he took seriously. The ring he bought for our 26th—on November 10, 1988—was a delicate little beauty. The accident was three days later.

When I went to drop him off at the Sea Island airport after dinner on November 13, I was upset because he and his two colleagues, Jimmy Hodges and John Popa, had chartered a big plane to fly them down to the Jacksonville airport and a little plane showed up instead. They couldn't even get all their golf clubs on the plane. They put the bags in my car and I was going to send the bags out on another plane later. I thought to myself, "Why don't I just drive them all down in a car?" No words can express how frustrating it is to have had that thought and not to have said anything, not to have done anything about it.

When Davis got into the plane, he did something odd. Although he had already kissed me goodbye, he came out of the plane, walked to the car and kissed me goodbye again. I never saw him again.

Our family was a foursome. Four golfers. Every foursome has a natural leader. Davis was our leader. After he died, we were a threesome. We all dealt with the changes in different ways. Mark, who is much like his father, quoted his father the morning after the accident. He said, "Whenever I did something wrong, Dad would say, 'All right, that's over and done. Let's go on from here and do the best we can.' And that's the way it has to be now." Those words helped, but I of course had my anger, my questions, my loneliness, long days, and sleepless nights. As for Davis III, he was grieving for all of us and at the same time trying to take care of all the day-to-day business and legal responsibilities, too. That was a heavy load for him.

Everybody responds to death differently. With the passing of time, I think Davis feels his father's presence more and more, not less and less. And I think the more he can feel his father's presence, the better he's going to be, on the course and off. After Davis's father died, Davis played with less joy, you could see that. He was playing out of a sense of obligation, as if to say, "This isn't going to be as much fun as it was when Dad was alive but this is what I have to do." Now I'm starting to see the joy come back. I think I've seen more and more of it since he won the Players Championship in 1992.

I think Davis would have been especially pleased that Mark was carrying Davis's bag at that tournament. When Mark caddied for Davis, he never felt that Mark was working for Davis; he thought of it as the boys playing together. He knew that Davis played better when Mark was caddying. After Davis Jr., there was nobody who knew Davis's game and swing and moods as well as Mark.

Davis always makes sure to include Mark in his triumphs. He'll say, "We were reading the wind and decided a nice regular 6-iron is all we'd need." They're a team.

I think Davis taught both his boys to show humility, to share, to realize that whatever you're doing you're not doing it alone. My husband was a modest man, but he knew when he had helped his students, and he agonized when he felt he hadn't. He wanted his students to call him if their game was off, whether it was his boys, or Peter Persons or Beth Daniel or *any* of his other students. Davis didn't think a teacher's personality should be central to the act of teaching the golf swing. Davis molded his personality to the personality of his pupil, came up with a language that would be meaningful to the student. He was never dismissive of another teacher; he listened to everything anybody had to say and wrote down on his legal pads any ideas of others he liked. Davis always said, "I'll learn from anyone." Davis was a natural teacher and a great communicator. He was my husband and my teacher. He was Mark's father and his teacher, teaching him how to teach. He was Davis's father and his teacher.

He was always learning and always teaching. On the afternoon of the accident, he was watching football on TV and I decided to go out to hit balls. I had a little invitational tournament to play in the next day. He said, "I'll come out with you." I said, "That's not necessary; stay and watch your football." But he turned off the television and came anyway.

After watching me hit a few shots he said, "Wow, I've never seen you hit the ball so well. Tell me what you're thinking." So I told him, "I have two of your thoughts and a third from Penick. The first is I want to feel my right thumb under the club at the top of my backswing. The second is I want to feel like I'm clipping the tee underneath the ball. And the third is I want to see three knuckles on my left hand at address."

He said, "That's good." He watched me hit a few more. "I think you've got something."

And I said, "I don't think I'll lose it now."

That lesson has stayed with me. When I go to a practice tee, I can still hear that conversation in my head. My golf is the same now as it was then; when it gets off kilter, I go back to that last lesson and I straighten myself out before too long. If I can't get it myself, Mark is my very able back-up teacher.

When Davis boarded that little plane at the Sea Island Airport, he carried a briefcase with a book inside it. Davis loved to read. He read mysteries and golf books—Davis III has his golf library today—but he was particularly interested in books that expanded the mind. In his briefcase was *The Power of Myth,* the transcript of a lengthy interview with Joseph Campbell, the philosopher, by Bill Moyers of PBS. The book deals with a lot of spiritual subjects. Although Davis grew up in the Presbyterian church, he was not a religious person, not in an outwardly way. But he was extremely interested in religion and spirituality. In fact, when we first started courting, he was reading a book about the great religions of the world. He was fascinated by the idea that most religions have as a basis some underlying premise, some form of the Golden Rule: Do unto others as you would have them do unto you. That's what guided his life. *The Power of Myth* fascinated Davis because it was about Joseph Campbell's search for Truth, and I write that with a capital T intentionally. Davis would read passages of the book out loud to me and say that I should read it, too. I said, "It might be a little deep for me." He said, "Just read a little at a time. Read it again and again until it makes sense."

Davis III retrieved Davis's copy of the book for me after the accident and I keep it on my nightstand today. Many times on sleepless nights I've reached for the book and found a great deal of comfort in it. The book communicates an important message for me. It says that the lessons of Truth are the lessons of God. My husband's life was about giving lessons. In every lesson he gave, he sought to find the truth, about his pupil and about himself.

Davis Jr. believed in family communication above all. When he was on the road, he called nightly. Once, when the boys were on the road, I chided them about calling during the day when the rates are at their highest. Davis said, "Penta, that's not an issue to be frugal about. If they have to wait, they may lose the chance to say what they want to say." To this day, I don't care how expensive our phone bills get. Mark and Davis are on the road a lot, just as their father was. They're good about calling.

Whenever their father was going on one of his trips, he'd say to Davis and to Mark, "Take care of your mother." They took his word literally; they learned his lessons well.

CHAPTER 10

Jack Lumpkin

After my father passed away, there was a long period of professional floundering for me. I played decently at times and horrendously at others. My swing was awful and I didn't know who to go to. I turned to Butch Harmon, an old friend of my father's, a member of a highly regarded golfing family and a superb teacher. (He coaches Tiger Woods, among many other leading players.) But Butch lives in Texas and I live in Sea Island, Georgia, and there wasn't that much opportunity to see one another. For the past few years my principal teacher has been Jack Lumpkin, and seeing Jack on a regular basis has been like coming home. Jack was an old and good friend of my father's. He and my father played the tour together a little bit before I was born. They helped each other get jobs. They worked together at the Golf Digest *schools. My father talked to Jack often about what he was trying to get me to do with my golf swing, and Jack watched me practice often when I was growing up. After my father died, Jack became the director of the Golf Learning Center at Sea Island. His style of teaching is different from my father's, but his goal is exactly the same. He wants to help each of his pupils to get all the satisfaction out of the game that they can. He's certainly doing that with me.*

JACK:

Davis Love Jr. was a teacher who didn't like to give a lot of explanation. He taught using as few words as possible. He believed in demonstrations and drills. He wanted a relaxed atmosphere, both in the golf swing and in the lesson itself. He thought of the swing as a motion. Once he had a student making a motion, his next job was to shape the motion. Once he shaped the motion, his next job was to get the motion to repeat. That's how simple he kept things. He said, "I'll trick 'em, if I can. I'll do anything I can to get the job done." I know he got a lot of that from Harvey Penick. He thought the world of Harvey. He'd tell me, "Jack, I want to be just like Harvey in every way, except one thing." And I'd say, "And what's that?" And he'd say, "I don't want to charge like Harvey." Harvey, you may know, gave a lot of lessons for free, and when he did charge it was never very much.

Davis was a very bright person. He was so bright that he didn't try to appear bright. And sometimes the very bright person can be a little high strung. He was very interested in the stock market and he was nervous as a cat if the stock market was doing one thing or another. He was most nervous whenever Davis III was playing; he was always running to phones between lessons to call press tents at tournaments to see how Davis was making out.

I think Davis Jr. had the most positive attitude of anyone I've ever known, and that attitude revealed itself particularly in his putting. When he played the tour he averaged about 27 putts per round and he did it with a kind of jabbing stroke that you could never use today, as fast as greens have become. But he was a great putter. I once asked Davis, "What would you do if you had 17 putts on the front side?" In other words, what would he do on a day when his stroke was really off through nine holes? I wanted to know what kind of adjustment he would make. Would he practice in front of a mirror between nines, talk sternly to his putter, take some practice strokes—what would he do? And Davis said, "I think I'd start walking real fast. I average 27 putts per round. I've already used 17? I'm going to have some *fun* on the back nine." And he could have nines where he one-putted nine greens; that's the kind of putter and chipper he was. He was famous for it. One time, Davis and I had a match against two old pros, Shelly Mayfield and Claude Harmon, who had won the Masters in 1948 and who was the head professional at Winged Foot. Before the match started Claude said, "I may not make any putts today, but I know I'll see some fall." He looked Davis in the eye when he said this.

Davis was a very organized person, very particular. When we'd go to a motel he'd make sure the room didn't overlook a highway or was near a soda machine. But sometimes he had these colossal gaps in his organization. Once, he went all the way to Spain for a *Golf Digest* School, arrived there, and realized that he didn't have his passport. They had to do all sorts of pleading to get him into the country, to assure the officials they could have his passport sent on the next plane, which they did. Another time, he drove up to the passenger drop-off at the airport in Jacksonville, got his bags out, got himself out, and went off to a school. When he came back, he toured all the parking lots looking for his car. Couldn't find it. He was very upset. So he went up to an airport official and said, "Who do I see about reporting a stolen car?"

And the man said, "What kind of car was it?"

"Yellow Lincoln," Davis said.

"Stolen? That car wasn't stolen. You left it right here in front, with the engine running, when you took the bags out." We kidded him unmercifully about that, because you didn't get to kid him often.

Davis and I were just about the same age; I was a half-year older, but he lost his hair early and I always kidded him about that.

When Davis was concentrating really hard on something, he'd flash his eyes back and forth, back and forth, really fast, deep in thought. You could see the wheels turning. So I'd say, "Davis, I know why you don't have any hair. You've burned out all the roots of your hair from the inside with all that eye-rolling you do when you're thinking about something."

But he was always thinking. I'd say to him, "Davis, you've got more ideas than anybody I know. The only thing is that for every seven ideas you have, only one is worth a damn. And the only reason you need me around is that I'm the guy who can pick out which one idea of your seven is any good." And he'd laugh.

He loved to laugh, and he loved to tell jokes. Not jokes in the conventional sense, more like very witty, insightful observations. He was wry. When he was starting as the head professional at the Atlanta Country Club, the club was brand new and they were building a pro shop. His first pro shop was in this little log cabin, down by the river. Then they built a clubhouse and they gave Davis a shop in the clubhouse. A year or so later they built a swimming pool and a director of the club came up to Davis and said, "Now someday, Davis, very soon, we're going to have a little shop where the lifeguards can sell bathing suits and whatnot, but in the meantime, would you mind if we devoted just a little corner of your golf pro shop to swimwear?" Davis of course was reluctant, but he said yes. A year later they built tennis courts, and a director of the club went back to Davis and said, "We're going to have a proper tennis pro shop at some point, it'll share space with the swim pro shop, but in the meantime, would you mind just taking a little corner of your shop and selling some tennis rackets and balls and tennis clothes?" Reluctantly, Davis said yes. The next day Davis put up a sign in front of his shop: "Davis Love: Specializing in backswings, backstrokes, and backhands."

A tour event, the old Atlanta Classic, is played at the Atlanta

Country Club, and in 1967 Davis got me a sponsor's exemption to play in the tournament. I was the head professional at Oak Hill, in Rochester, New York, at the time, and it was a big thrill for me, since I'm from Athens, Georgia. It was a chance to play in front of my friends and family. I told Davis how much I appreciated the exemption, and Davis said, "Happy to do it. Now why don't you get me a sponsor's exemption for your tournament next year?" Well, my tournament the next year was the U.S. Open! There was no way I could get Davis an exemption for the Open, and he knew it—but Davis qualified his way in, anyhow. He played in a lot of majors.

When he was playing he was often nervous. He'd get nervous and then he'd start bumming cigarettes from caddies, spectators, playing partners, just about anybody. Penta didn't want him to smoke and he was always trying to quit, but without much success. The one thing he did, like a lot of people who are trying to quit, is to not buy cigarettes. He just bummed them. One time we were doing a Golf School at Pinehurst and we had a banquet with the students to mark the conclusion, as we always do. The students gave Davis two packs of cigarettes, for all the cigarettes he bummed. Davis held up the two packs of cigarettes and said, "Would you look at this? They come in packs now." He broke them up with that.

But he took the golf schools seriously, not only because they paid him his living, but because he really cared about his students getting better in golf. At one *Golf Digest* School we had Sam Snead coming, which was exciting. Before Sam arrived, Davis laid down some rules with him. He said, "Sam, no cursing with these students."

"No cursing?" Sam said. "Damn."

"And I don't want you telling any of your jokes, because they're all off-color."

"Did I ever tell you the one about the lady in the purple tights—"

"And, Sam, I don't want you making fun of these students," Davis told Sam. He was worried about that. Sam was the kind of guy who might say to a lousy player, "First thing you do is stop playing for two weeks. Then you stop playing altogether."

So Sam looked at Davis and said, "Well, Davis, what exactly am I supposed to do at this thing?"

And Davis said, "Hit pretty golf shots, because that's what you do best." Davis was quite serious when he said it, even though he was talking to a golfing legend. He was laying it on the line with Sam Snead.

But there was nothing in golf Davis took more seriously than the golfing development of his two sons. I think one of the few mistakes Davis ever made, and we talked about this before he died, was letting Mark follow Davis to the University of North Carolina. When Mark got there as a freshman he was a very good player, but Davis was already a star and I think it was hard for Mark to find his own way. Much was expected of Mark, maybe more than he could do. In the end, it worked out fine, because Mark is a fine young man and he helps Davis with his game a great deal and he's learning so much about golf being out on tour; if he ever wants to be a full-time teacher he's going to have great experiences to fall back on. Those experiences will help his teaching immeasurably. Mark can do just about anything he wants to do in the game.

Davis Jr. and I talked a lot about Davis III, which is why, I suppose, I'm his teacher today. Davis would have me watch Davis III hit balls, but I would never talk directly to Davis III. I wanted Davis Jr. to screen whatever thoughts I had. We felt it was important for Davis to have one teacher. There was only one time that I saw something when Davis wanted me to tell it directly to Davis III. He said to me, "Go ahead, tell him yourself." So I did, and we worked on one change, small but significant—I felt his left arm was getting too far away from his chest—and he hit every last ball we could find until dusk came. And then the next week, he won his first tour event, at Hilton Head, in 1987. So I felt that maybe I had made a little contribution to that victory, which is a nice feeling.

After Davis Jr. died, I told Davis that his father said to me, "I know that Davis should make some changes in his swing over time, and I know he will." And I said to Davis, "You need to find a really good teacher. I'm not suggesting it has to be me, although I'd be honored and delighted to do it. I'd just ask that whomever you choose, maybe you and I and your teacher and I can talk from time to time, so I can filter it a little bit, from what I think your dad would say." Then two months after Davis died I came to Sea Island, basically to take Davis's job. For a while Butch Harmon, the son of Claude Harmon, who was my old boss at Winged Foot, would watch Davis on tour, and I'd help him out a little at home. Butch and I would talk, to make sure we were giving him basically the same thing.

At the end of the 1994 season, Davis and I had a talk and he said, "I need to rededicate myself to the game. I'm not in the Masters, I missed the Tour championship, I'm not on the Ryder Cup team, I didn't win a tournament last year, I've fallen from second to 12th to 33rd on the money list. I don't like it. What are we going to do about it?" And my essential thought was that he wasn't working as hard on his game as he had been. So I said, "Davis, you got some time?" And he said, "Sure." So we went out and had a four-hour lesson. And we'd never spent that kind of time on a single lesson before. At the end of four hours Davis said, "Well, that gives me some things to think about, some things to work on. When do we meet again?" And I said, "Tomorrow morning at 9 A.M." So then we had another four-hour session. And I think, or I hope, that that got Davis thinking about how important it is to really throw yourself into what you're doing. That was my point, anyhow. Golf has always come very easily for Davis. Maybe too easily.

Then, in 1995, he won in New Orleans and finished second in the Masters. In 1996 he won in San Diego and finished second in the U.S. Open. They were two good years. They could have been two great years. They could have been player-of-the-year years. He's close.

Every time I teach Davis I'm always very aware that he is not an ordinary student. He is Davis Love III, son of Davis Love, Jr., and I think it's important that he have the swing his dad gave him. If his dad could see Davis's swing today he'd say, "That's the swing he's always had." But he would also say, "It's matured nicely. It's a better swing than it used to be." At least I hope and think that's what he would say.

When I'm teaching Davis, I'm very careful not to say to him, "Your dad used to say this." I don't think he needs a constant stream of reminders about his dad. He has a lot of that going on as it is. But every once in a while I'll see him do something and I know how his father would respond, so I just have to tell him. One time Davis and I were playing and he was trying to make this very-low-percentage shot with a driver off the ground to a green that was about 290 yards away, and there was water and marsh all along the flight line of the ball. Davis was playing those new Titleists, the Professional, which cost about five dollars a ball. And he hit one in the water. And then another. And then another. And after I'd seen about enough of that I said, "If your dad was here he'd say, 'You can tell Davis isn't paying for those balls himself at five dollars apiece, because if he was he'd have done the sensible thing and hit an iron out and a wedge on a long time ago.'"

But when you see Davis try a shot like that you know it's his competitiveness getting the better of him. It's an internal competitiveness, which all great golfers have. His father had it in the exact same way. When Davis was at the Atlanta Country Club and I was at Oak Hill we used to have matches between our two clubs in February. We'd come to Sea Island and it would be Davis and three members from his club against me and three members from my club. The first three years we had this event, Davis's team won. Then in the fourth year, my team was winning after two days of play. We were going into the third and final day and the weather was awful. It was a driving rain and the wind was blowing about 30 miles an hour and it was cold. The course was closed. Davis was saying, "I don't know why they won't let us play, it's a beautiful day." He didn't want to lose this match. He said, "I know I could go out and shoot 35 for nine myself today." So this gets us all going, and all sorts of money is being bet on whether Davis can shoot 35 or not. Davis got permission to play. And we decided that if Davis could shoot 35 or better, his team would win, and if not, Oak Hill would win.

We get to the first hole, and that's normally about a driver and a 6-iron for him. But on this day, with the wind in his face, it's a driver and a 3-wood, which he hits 40 feet short of the hole. He holes out that putt for a three, so he's one under after one. On the second hole, Davis hits a driver on a 420-yard hole. His second shot is off an upslope, from a grassy lie. He holes it. So now he's gone birdie-eagle. He's three under after two. There had been more than two dozen people following him around. After that, there was about one left. Everybody said, "He's going to win the bet." And he did. He shot 34. At dinner that night he said, "I thought the course was very playable today." I could see Davis III saying that same sort of thing today.

Davis Jr. was always there to guide Davis III, but he never forced things on him. He let Davis find things for himself. He knew that the things somebody told you had some value, but the things you learned for yourself had an immense value. He wanted to give Davis just enough of the facts so that he could figure out the rest for himself. I try to do that with Davis III. The more Davis can figure out for himself the more self-reliant he becomes, which has to be the goal of all teachers, even if it means putting yourself out of a job. Davis Jr. wanted Davis to be self-reliant and he was moving Davis in that direction when he died. Of course, Davis's death was totally unexpected and Davis III was not ready to fly solo at the time. The death really crushed him. Any time a parent dies it's crushing, but for Davis it was a particularly cruel blow. He had always assumed that he could always come home and his father would be there and have all the answers to his problems. The truth is that Davis did have a lot of the answers, but nobody has all the answers, and it has taken Davis III a long time to figure that out. But I think he has. I think the realization that he is obligated to figure things out for himself has made him a better golfer and a better person. If Davis Jr. had lived, things might have been considerably different. Davis III might have played much better. He might have won more. But you don't know. Davis's death made Davis III tougher, more determined. And succeeding in tournament golf is, ultimately, about being really tough and really determined. Davis is, now; you can see that in his Ryder Cup play, in how he prepares for the majors, how he plays in them. When he wins them, he'll be winning them for his father, and for himself. It will be the cumulation of everything. That's why golf is so interesting. That's why a man as bright as Davis Love Jr. wanted to devote his life to it, and have his sons devote their lives to it, too.

CONTROL YOUR WEDGES

So many 15-handicappers can get within 30 to 50 yards of the green in regulation and then can't leave themselves with a reasonable putt for par. The reason for that is poor wedge play. These golfers are good enough to make a good, clean hit with the wedge, get the ball airborne, get it to land softly. What they seem to struggle with is how far to hit the wedge. They can't control their distance. My father had a remedy for that; he'd say, "Control the distance on your wedge shots with the length of your backswing, not with the speed of your swing." That requires practice, so that you know how far back you need to bring the clubhead in order to fly the ball a certain distance. But once that's part of your muscle memory, your trouble with wedge shots should be diminished. The speed is always the same. What changes is how far back your hands go.

AN UNDERHAND TOSS

My dad was one of those guys who would sometimes pretend to throw a ball underhand with his right hand before playing a bunker shot or a chip or a pitch, to get a feel for the softness the shot required, the ease with which it would come off the clubhead, the way it would roll across the green. You might find such an approach useful for yourself. He took that same idea to practicing those shots, particularly little pitching wedge shots. To learn to hit them high and soft, he encouraged his players to practice pitch shots with just the right hand. It's the right hand that slides the face of the wedge under the ball. While the left arm is the true creator of the swing—that is an axiom—the fine-tuning is done with the right.

GET IT ROLLING

My father didn't believe much in edicts, but he did believe in systems. For example, with regard to chipping, his catch phrase, as it was for all the other instructors in the *Golf Digest* Schools, was "Minimum air time, maximum ground time." When chipping, mistakes are more likely to occur with the ball in the air than on the ground. Generally speaking, it's better to chip with a 7-iron than a pitching wedge. It's often better to "chip" with a putter than a 7-iron. Maximize your ground time. As fairway grasses have become finer and finer, and cut shorter and shorter, putting from around the green has increasingly become an option you see players on tour choosing. There's a lot of truth to the old saying, "A poor putt is better than a poor chip."

A HANDFUL OF SAND

An important part of making good greenside bunker shots is to visualize how the sand will fly when you make your swing. Dad's advice here was to look at the ball and pretend you were going to throw a handful of sand from right behind the ball onto the green. That's a very useful image, because it's soft and graceful. My father didn't like the phrase "explosion shot." He'd be mad at me now for even bringing up the phrase. There's an ease to the well-played bunker shot. It doesn't require a bit of brute force.

THE BURIED BUNKER SHOT

Everybody always says that the buried bunker shot is one of the toughest in golf, and that faced with such a shot a player's prospects are so dim that he should just be thrilled to be able to scrape the ball out of the bunker. The time-honored method for such an extraction was to close the face, aim a couple of inches behind the ball, and swing as hard as you can. And to all of that, my father would say, "Nonsense." He believed that a buried bunker shot could be played properly *only* with an open face because that is the only way to control the ball. So the next question, naturally, is, "How do you play a bunker shot from a buried lie with an open face, so that you may control the ball?" There are two answers, really: Hit the ball a little harder, with a fuller follow-through than you would for a normal bunker shot, taking more sand and allowing for extra roll, because of the extra topspin. The second answer is the same answer the man gets when asking how to get to Carnegie Hall: "Practice, practice, practice."

A MATCH FOR ANYONE

Dad used to say, as Harvey Penick did before him, "A man who can putt and chip is a match for anyone; a man who can't is a match for no one." Which is another way of saying, "You drive for show, you putt for dough." Believe it or not, there are a bunch of players, on the tour and in college, who can hit the ball as long as Tiger Woods; there are a few who can hit it longer. The reason

Tiger Woods is Tiger Woods is because his game is not just driving the ball immense distances. He can putt and chip. If he couldn't, you wouldn't know his name. That's not to say he can putt and chip with, say, Corey Pavin. Not yet, anyway. Corey probably putts and chips as well as anybody who has ever played the game, and as a result, he can play with anyone. If Corey and Tiger played 10 consecutive head-to-head matches on U.S. Open courses, my guess is that Corey would win six or seven of them, even though Tiger would blow some of his drives 100 yards past Corey's. Why do I say this? Because a man who can putt and chip is a match for anyone.

A MATCH-PLAY TIP

In match play, one thing you can do that will always get your opponent thinking is to take out the flagstick when you're chipping. Not that that's a reason to do it, but your opponent surely knows, as my father always said, "If you think you can hole a chip shot out, take out the flagstick, because the flagstick never helped a perfect shot." Having said that, I think it's often wise to leave the flagstick in. How often, after all, are perfect shots hit? If the shot is downhill, or out of a bunker, I'll always leave the flagstick in.

LEAVE IT TO PHIL

If there was one part of my game that really irritated my father, it was my tendency to "flip" at my wedge shots—that is, to play wedge shots with a great deal of wrist. A lot of good golfers like to play shots with a very wristy, handsy action. It's fun, it lets you show off how much you can spin the ball, it's a wordless comment on your eye–hand coordination. The one thing it's not is reliable. In general, the more you can take the little muscles and body parts out of the swing—your wrists and hands specifically—and the more you can rely on the big muscles and body parts—your quadriceps and shoulders specifically—the more repeatable your swing will be.

In 1986, when I first got on tour, a lot of players were taking a fairway wood or a long iron out of their bags for the first time in order to carry a third wedge, often called a lob wedge. A lob wedge, generally, has 60 degrees of loft, more loft than a sand wedge. Dad applauded my decision to put a third wedge in my bag; since the club had more loft to it, I didn't have to "create" loft by hitting wristy shots. I believe every golfer should have a club in his bag that he can hit 30 to 60 yards without making an exaggerated, handsy swing. For most golfers, that club is the lob wedge. You might be thinking: But what about all those magical handsy little wedge shots that Phil Mickelson plays so beautifully? I'd suggest you leave them to Phil. I do, and so do most of my touring brethren. A more reliable recipe is this: Wrists out; lob wedge in.

CHAPTER 11

Harvey's Boys

Golfers are often praised for calling penalties on themselves, but I don't think there's anything honorable in it. It's basic, and the overwhelming majority of my touring brethren think the same. A golf course typically occupies about 150 acres. In the first two rounds of a tournament, there are usually 150 or so players. Given the size of the playing field and the number of players on it, golfers must monitor their own play, as a practical consideration. But more to the point, golfers policing their own play is the thread that holds the entire tradition of the game together. Golf is special, unique among most modern professional sports, because it remains gentlemanly; it continues to value courtesy for one's opponent. I think every serious golfer knows, regardless of what kind of boor he might be off the course, that golf would not be the game it is if players failed to call rules violations on themselves. Of the several hundred different tour players I've played with over the years, I cannot imagine more than one or two of them willfully breaking the rules. At most tour events, more than 40,000 shots are played over the course of four rounds, and most weeks *all* of them are played as the rules require. I have never witnessed an instance of intentional cheating, and I have witnessed dozens of occasions in which golfers have called penalties on themselves. When these occasions receive public accolades, I'm reminded of what Bobby Jones used to say: "Don't praise me for calling a penalty on myself. You might as well praise a man for not robbing a bank."

My strangest instance of calling a penalty on myself came in the 1994 Western Open at Cog Hill, outside Chicago. It was strange because I did not know—and still don't—if I did something wrong or not. But the rule book is clear: If you think it's possible that you have committed an infraction, and nobody else is in a position to judge the case, then you *have* committed an infraction. This may sound harsh to the nongolfer, but it's not. Adhered to strictly, it eliminates the possibility of a golfer playing with a guilty conscience.

For the first two rounds of the 1994 Western, I was paired with Tom Watson and Andrew Magee. I opened with a 71 and was going along fine in the second round when I arrived at the 13th hole, a par four. I put my second shot in the bunker and then nearly holed my bunker shot. The ball finished about a foot from the hole. Life is good.

My ball had sand on it, so rather than just tap it in I marked my ball with a small coin. Then I realized that the coin was in the line of Watson's putt, so I moved it, as the rules allow, the length of a putterhead. Magee had already holed out. Watson then drained his birdie putt and those two guys were off to the 14th tee. While they were marching off, I put my ball down and tapped in for my four and then followed them to the next hole.

I hit my tee shot on 14, and while walking down the fairway a sickening feeling came over me: I could not remember if I had returned my mark to its original position, as the rules require, and tapped in from there, or if had I putted out from the place to which I had moved the mark. The latter situation would result in a two-stroke penalty. I turned to my caddie, Frank Williams, and asked if he could remember. Frank is one of the best caddies on tour; when Tiger Woods turned pro and was asking about caddies, I recommended Frank to him. But he doesn't have eyes in the back of his head, and while I was putting he was raking the bunker; he didn't know if I had returned the mark to its original position. My two playing partners and their caddies did not see me hole out, either. I told Magee, who was keeping my scorecard, that my score on 13 was a six, not a four, after adding a two-stroke penalty for failing, or for the possibility of failing, to return my ball to its original position.

When we came out of the scorer's tent, Watson said to me, "Good luck on the weekend." That's the customary wish playing partners from the first two rounds say to one another, provided they've made the 36-hole cut.

"I'm not playing on the weekend," I told Watson. "I'm going to miss the cut."

"How does 144 not play on the weekend?" Watson said. Watson knows all the numbers, what he shot, what you shot, what the guy in the group in front of him shot, what the cut will be, how many under the leader is. Watson knew that the cut at the Western was likely to be 145, which it was. He has a head for numbers.

"I shot 75 today for 146. I had a two-stroke penalty on 13 when I couldn't remember if I moved my mark back to its original position."

Watson gave me a look and a shrug, but no sympathy. None was called for. In golf, you're responsible for the sanctity of your card, and every golfer knows it.

Months later, writer John Feinstein pointed out to me that had I made the cut at the Western Open and finished in the middle of the pack, I would have earned $5,000. Add $5,000 to my 1994 earnings and I would have finished among the top 30 on the money list, instead of 33rd. The top 30 money winners at the close of one season receive automatic invitations to the following year's Masters. But I was not among the top 30 money winners. There would be no engraved invitations with Augusta postmarks arriving in my mailbox. I've been praised for my honesty, and that's nice, but the truth is there's no decision to make. Let's say I didn't call the penalty on myself, I did finish among the top 30, I went to the Masters and won. That win would have been totally fraudulent.

By finishing the 1994 season 33rd on the money list, there was only one way for me to get an invitation for the 1995 Masters: I had to win one of the 13 events of the 1995 season played prior to the Masters. That was a powerful motivator.

If you look at the records of the dominant players of this era—Tom Watson, Nick Faldo, Greg Norman, Bernhard Langer—they play in the four major tournaments year after year. They're following in the footsteps of Jack Nicklaus. In his prime, Jack used to say, "I set my calendar by the majors." But after 1994, I couldn't do the same. I wasn't in the Masters, I wasn't in the U.S. Open. I hadn't earned a place on the Ryder Cup team. After two big years in 1992 and 1993, I didn't do anything of real note in 1994. It was in the off-season, at the end of 1994 and before the start of 1995, that I turned myself over to Jack Lumpkin and made him my primary swing coach. I told Jack that I didn't want to go back out on tour until my game was in the kind of shape it needed to be to win again, and that when I did go back out I was going to be hell-bent on winning. I *despised* the idea of not playing at Augusta.

I didn't go out until Phoenix, the fourth tournament of the year. The next week, at Pebble Beach, I tied for third. Good, but not good enough. The next week, at San Diego, I finished in a tie for 12th. I skipped the Hope, played nothing special at the Los Angeles Open, but was feeling good about my game as the tour began again on the East Coast. At Doral, I finished in a tie for fourth. I didn't play at the Honda, then at Bay Hill finished in a tie for 16th.

I was making money, but I was running out of chances. All that was left was the Players Championship and New Orleans. At the Players Championship, I was tied for the lead through 70 holes of the tournament, then I knocked my tee shot in the water on 17, and in the end finished three shots back. On to New Orleans. New Orleans was the last stop.

I played the first two rounds in New Orleans with Ben Crenshaw, who had won the tournament the previous year. I opened with a 68 and followed that with a 69. "Man, are you ever playing good," Ben said. (Tour players, even highly literate ones like Ben Crenshaw, will often use *good* for *well,* especially if they're from Texas.) Ben was struggling. His toe was bothering him and he felt he couldn't make a proper swing and he was driving the ball erratically. He missed the cut by four shots. His game was all over the place. Even his vaunted putting game was ill. He was so frustrated with his flat stick that he started putting with an iron on the last three or four holes. The greens at the English Turn Golf & Country Club, where the tournament is played, are reminiscent of the greens at Augusta, lightning fast with incredible slopes. I wondered what Ben would do to get his game ready for the Masters, which would be played the next week. He didn't seem particularly concerned; Harvey Penick, his mentor and teacher, was in very ill health and Ben was distracted.

Come Saturday, I knew it was time for me to go low if I was going to win the tournament. At tournaments where the winning score is going to be a load under par, you pretty much have to shoot a low number on Saturday to put yourself in position to win on Sunday. If you're going to have one really low round in a week, you'd rather have it on a Saturday or Sunday than a Thursday or Friday. For instance, in the 1994 Hawaiian Open I shot 60, with an eagle on the last hole, in the second round, on a Friday. Anytime you shoot 12 under it's helpful, but I wish the round would have come on a day beginning with *S.* It's tough to improve on a 60. It gave me a four shot lead, but I still had 36 holes to think about what I was doing right on Friday and what I was doing wrong, by comparison, on Saturday and Sunday. There's such a thing as having too much time on your hands. I shot 71–71 on the weekend to finish a stroke back of the winner, Brett Ogle. If you're a religious reader of golf scores in the newspapers, you'll find that players who shoot really low scores in either of the first two rounds seldom win the tournament. Anyway, to get back to the last stop on the train to Augusta, in the third round in New Orleans I went low. My 66 was the best score in the field. At the end of three rounds, I had a one-shot lead over Mike Standly and Steve Jones.

The last round was incredibly nerve-racking. Not only was I trying to win the tournament, I was trying to get into the Masters, too. I couldn't separate one goal from the other. On Sunday, in the final round, I was nicely in control of my game through 16. My lead was a shot or two pretty much the whole day. I saved my bone-headed play for the end: a bogey on 17 and another on 18. Instead of winning the tournament outright, I had played my way into a playoff with Mike Heinen. Agony.

Up to that point in my career, I had been in three playoffs and lost all three of them. Tom Kite beat me in 1989 at Bay Hill. Tom Purtzer beat me in 1991 at the World Series of Golf. Freddy Couples beat me in 1992 at Los Angeles, where he is king. I knew that people were saying I couldn't win playoffs because I was too nice. (And in 1996, I was in two more playoffs without winning.) I've always felt that that criticism was absurd, although it is true that Ben Crenshaw, who is the nicest man on earth, had been in eight playoffs through the end of 1996, and had won none. But it was time for me to be merciless. Mike and I both made pars on the first playoff hole. On the second, the 190-yard par-3 17th that I'd bogeyed a couple of minutes earlier, I stiffed my tee shot. Mike made a good par from the fringe, I holed my birdie putt, and minutes later, by a fax sent to the press tent at New Orleans, I received my invitation to the 1995 Masters. My joy was immense.

It was also short-lived. Flying home, with Robin and my mother, Mom said to me, "Davis, I'm afraid I have some sad news. Harvey passed away this afternoon."

I wept uncontrollably. I was inconsolable. Harvey Penick had led a good life, a great life. He was ninety. His death was by no means unexpected. My weeping was for my father, and for the order of the deaths. Harvey was like a father to my father. The son is supposed to bury the father; that's the natural sequence. With Harvey's death, my father's passing was immediate and fresh again. With Harvey alive, I felt my father was, in some indescribable way, alive too. I felt part of my father lived on through Harvey. With Harvey's death, the last link was gone. With Harvey gone, my father's death was more real to me than it had ever been before. With Harvey gone, I was filled with regret. I knew Harvey, I had spent time with Harvey, I had taken lessons from Harvey. But I hadn't done enough. Once, Harvey saw me on TV trying to charge a putt on the last hole to win a tournament. He knew my normal putting method was to let the ball fall in gently from the front of the cup. He knew because that was the putting method he taught my father and the one my father taught me. He called me on the phone after seeing my too-bold putt and said, "You must putt on the last hole precisely as you putt on the first." After that, I should have boarded a plane to Austin to see him. I wish I had. In the years after my father's death, I could have sought him out, really spent time with him, really gotten to know him. I didn't, and now that chance was gone.

Robin had been talking about having a party when we arrived home, to celebrate the New Orleans win before I left for Augusta. After I learned about Harvey's death, I told her to cancel the party.

"But people won't understand," she said. "You tell them that Mr. Penick has passed away, they'll understand," I said. When I got home, my first call was to Tom Kite, a close friend of Harvey's. Tom's wife, Christy, answered the phone. I couldn't get any words out. I later learned that minutes before Harvey died, Tom was at Harvey's bedside, telling him about the result of the playoff in New Orleans. Mr. Penick was too weak to speak, but he brought his hands together and made a whisper of a clap. A short while later, he drew his final breath.

I left for Augusta feeling very melancholic and a little lost. The one thing that had been in good shape was my game, but that seemed to be slipping away on me. On the practice tee at Augusta, Jack Lumpkin and I were working together and I was struggling. Sam Snead stopped by and watched me hit a few. "I watched you on TV in New Orleans, saw how you finished there," Sam said, talking about my bogey-bogey collapse on the 71st and 72nd holes. "Boy, are you quittin' on the ball. You're just getting in close to the ball and collapsing. Swing on through, son. Keep that club going out and up." Generally, at this point in my golfing development, when something goes wrong with my swing I need advice that is a little more technical than what Sam was saying. But the thing about the golf swing is, and the reason why my father listened to anybody who had a thought about the swing, you never know what or when something's going to click. When a Sam Snead takes the time to tell you something, anything, you listen. "Out and up" became a swing key for me for that week at Augusta. Right there in front of Sam I started hitting some good shots again.

I wanted to attend Harvey's funeral, which was held the day before the first round of the Masters, but to be wholly truthful I dreaded the idea, too. I knew there would be a lot of people there—old friends of my father's from his University of Texas days, old colleagues of his from the *Golf Digest* Schools—and seeing them all assembled would make me feel like I was at Dad's funeral again. That thought petrified me. On the other hand, I was eager to show my respect for Harvey, and to pay my respects to his wife, Helen, and son, Tinsley. I asked Ben Crenshaw, who was making arrangements to get back to Austin for the funeral, what I should do.

"The way you're playing, you've got a very good chance to win here," Ben said. "The way I'm playing, it doesn't matter what I do. Harvey would want you to stay and practice and get yourself ready for the tournament. Your father would say the same. I'll pass along your wishes to Helen and Tinsley."

The Masters was important to my father, whether he was playing in it or watching it. The golf course of the Augusta National Golf Club put Southern golf on the map. Growing up, the Masters was part of my heritage. Ben's words revealed an immense understanding of me and my dad, and I will always be grateful to him for what he said.

I finally had a good Masters. With rounds of 69, 69, and 71 I was in striking range through 54 holes, three shots back of the leaders, Brian Henninger and, lo and behold, Ben Crenshaw. There was all sorts of talent at the top of the leaderboard: Scott Hoch, Jay Haas, Steve Elkington, Freddy Couples, and Phil Mickelson were all one shot back. Curtis Strange was two shots back. Greg Norman was tied with me. The golf course owed something to Curtis, Greg, and Scott, all of whom have had victory snatched from them there. It was anybody's tournament to win. I shot the low round of the day on Sunday, a 66. I was the leader in the clubhouse or, more specifically, Butler Cabin, where I was holed away with Jack Stephens, the chairman of the tournament, feeling very, very content. I felt that one of Harvey's boys—Ben or me—would win the tournament. I was in a position to enjoy watching Ben play home. By the time I caught up with Ben on the television in the cabin, where the winner is presented with his green coat, Ben was on the 16th tee. He needed to play the final three holes in level par to tie me and force a playoff. I had pictures in my mind of the two of us walking down the hill from the 10th tee in a playoff. He needed to play the final three holes in one under par to beat me.

That's exactly what he did. He holed incredible putts on 16 and 17 for birdie, and by the time he got to 18 all he needed was a bogey to win, which is what he made, for a closing 68. To see him win the Masters, to see him consoled in his joy and his grief by his wonderful caddie, Carl Jackson, was, to me, one of the great moments in golf history. I was proud to play a small part in it. I could not have been happier for Ben, or for the game. With Ben's win, I felt Harvey's legacy was now twice assured. As long as golf is played, people will be reading Harvey's ingenious *Little Red Book.* As long as there are grill rooms, people will be telling the story of how Ben Crenshaw—with his game adrift, with the Texas dirt on his mentor's coffin still fresh—found his game and made his peace and won his second Masters. I have often wondered about the phrase "divine intervention." Ben's win at Augusta made me a believer.

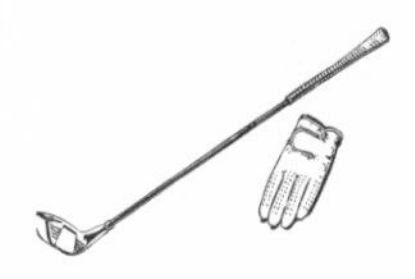

LOOKS DON'T COUNT

In assembling my father's notes to help with this book, I noticed he had hundreds upon hundreds of pages devoted to the swing, to practice techniques, to mental aspects of the game, and relatively few devoted to putting. That's because putting, he believed, was one area of the game that allowed for real idiosyncrasies. Some people look at Ben Crenshaw putt and say, "How can he putt standing that tall?" Well, the answer is pretty obvious to anybody who watched the 1995 Masters. Some people look at Jack Nicklaus and say, "How could he putt, so crouched over the ball?" Well, that answer's pretty clear to anyone who saw the 1986 Masters. Some people say, "How could Arnold Palmer putt so well, with his body twisted like a pretzel as he stands over the ball?" Well, that answer is evident to anybody who witnessed the 1958 Masters. My father said the most important thing about a putting stance is that it be natural *for you.* A natural stance is a necessary first step to a flowing stroke. Putting, more than any other aspect of the game, is about highly individual trial and error. There is one basic, though. If you ask my wife, who doesn't play golf—well, she plays if, say, Barbara Nicklaus is having a charity event and the golfer's wives will play and the husbands will caddie—what single golf tip she remembers from my father, she'll tell you she remembers only one: The head of the putter must follow through to the hole. (Or, when the putt is not straight, the follow-through must be on the intended line of the putt.) Follow-throughs that finish to the left, or to the right, are putts that have no chance, unless you're incredibly lucky.

By the way, if you're ever lucky enough to stay overnight at one of the cottages on the Augusta National property, you'll find that television there is like no place else. All you have to do is pick up the phone, call the front desk and say, "I'd like to watch the '58 Masters, please." Moments later, it's on your TV. I've seen a lot of holed putts during my stays there, and many of them have come from unusual stances. Nearly all have come from straight follow-throughs.

GIVE LUCK A CHANCE

One of my father's favorite Harvey Penick sayings was, "Give luck a chance." That means that when putting, get the ball to the front edge of the hole and see if it might fall in. A slow-moving putt that touches the lip of the hole has a chance to fall in; a putt that's flying as it passes the hole has no chance. People say, "Davis, why aren't you bolder with those 12-footers?" If I miss a 12-footer, I'd rather have the ball sitting on the edge of the hole so I can finish it off with a simple tap-in than have to do all sorts of work for 40 inches coming back. When playing partners would say to Bobby Jones, "Never up, never in," he'd say, "I've never seen a putt that went past the hole that went in, either."

A WIDE LANE

Some people imagine the line of a putt to be terribly thin, like a pencil line. My father, who was a wonderful putter despite a very jabby stroke that he would teach to no one, believed that the line of a putt was more like a highway stripe, as thick as a golf hole. It's easier to think of it that way, because then you don't have to make a perfect stroke for the ball to go in. You have over two inches to play with. Just get it generally on line, with the right speed, and a putt has a chance to fall in.

READING GREENS

I once asked my father why some people were good at reading greens and others were not. He said, "Because some people *practice* reading greens and others do not." Reading greens takes practice. When you're on a practice green, don't just figure out the break by taking a few putts; give the putt a read first, then confirm or disprove your read with a putt. That will help you develop the skill you need to read greens and give you confidence once you're on the course that you know what you're doing.

There are many, many different things that go into reading a putt, many of them incredibly subtle, like the direction of the wind, the direction the grass is growing, which way the cup tilts; in time and with practice you can develop the skills necessary to read greens expertly. But the biggest consideration is what the old tour caddie, the late Lee Lynch, used to call "overhaul" break. The overall break, the prevailing tendency of a green, can be determined by imagining sheets of rain falling on the green. As the water runs off the green, in which direction is it going? That's the way the green breaks, and it's often the way the grain grows, too. Greens are designed to drain water.

"I PUTT AS I DRIVE"

Percy Boomer, the great golf instructor from the first half of this century, said, "I putt as I drive." A lot of golfers struggle with this thought; they think that the swing with the driver and the swing with the putter are radically different, but they're not. The golfer who takes his putterhead outside the intended line on the backswing is likely to take the clubhead outside the intended line on the backswing with the driver. The golfer who quits on his follow-through with the driver is likely to do the same with the putter. I mention both those problems because they're so common and because my father dealt with both of them.

To make sure his pupils weren't going outside the line when

putting, he put down a 2 x 4 parallel to the line of the student's putt, with the leading edge of the board even with the ball. If you took the putterhead outside, you'd crash into the board. On the follow-through, he'd put a tee in the ground several inches ahead of the ball, just off the line of the putt, and make sure that the putterhead got past the tee on follow-through. Once those thoughts are ingrained in one's putting stroke, it's easier to incorporate them into your long game. Funny thing, though: My father taught a flowing putting stroke, and hid his own jab-stroke from his pupils. A prime illustration of, "Do as I say, not as I do."

PRACTICE YOUR STROKE

A useful quote from my father's notebooks: "To practice your putting *stroke,* practice with no target in mind." That will get you thinking just about the flow of your arms through the ball and get you away from worries about whether practice putts are falling to the bottom of the hole or not. Get the stroke sweet and smooth and the putts will drop.

THE ELEVEN-CENT DRILL

A very common mistake when putting is to strike the top half of the ball on a descending blow, creating a bumpy roll. Really good putters are seldom given enough credit for the quality of their roll, how the ball rolls end over end. That's what keeps a putt on line, and that's why good putters hole more putts than ordinary putters. My father had a drill to promote a good strike with the putter. He'd place a penny on the ground—on a green if at a course, on a carpet if he was inside—and place a dime on top of the penny. Then he'd have us make strokes in which we would knock the dime off the penny while leaving the penny in place. That teaches you to make contact slightly on the upswing and not at the bottom of the ball.

This drill really works. One of the things I remember most clearly from my youth is my father saying to me, while giving a lesson, "Hey, Davis—do me a favor and run into the pro shop and get me a dime and a penny." Dad never grew tired of that drill—and never learned to carry the necessary coins in his pocket, either.

DOCTOR'S ORDERS

Dad was a firm believer in going to experts for expert advice. Once we went to see Cary Middlecoff, who was widely considered to be the best putter of his day. Dr. Middlecoff said something along the lines of this: "After you stroke a putt, the only thing you can do is listen for it to fall in. You're not going to gain anything by peeking." For some reason, I forget to do this for periods at a time, and when I go back to it it always helps my putting.

Dr. Middlecoff gave me two other excellent putting suggestions. He had me stand a little more hunched over the ball, which is how he stood, and he and I were both tall and thin. He said, "I like to see a golfer close to his work." He also said that standing less tall would get me "out of the wind." That may sound silly, but any golfer, and a tall golfer in particular, can get blown around while standing over a putt, and that's a killer. The other thing he said was to close my stance a little on a hooking putt, a putt that breaks from right to left, and open my stance a little on a slicing putt, a putt that breaks from left to right. He said, "Cheat a little to the right on the right-to-lefters," and "Cheat a little to the left on the left-to-righters." Why he called that cheating, I couldn't tell you for sure. Probably because he thought it made putting a little easier, and anything you can do in golf to make it easier seems like cheating, even when it's not.

PRACTICE ON LINE

One of the things that made my father such a successful teacher was that he saw some very basic mistakes in the most common of practices. For instance, the vast majority of golfers, when taking a practice putting stroke, stroke the practice putt directly at the hole. Wrong! The practice putting stroke should be exactly parallel to the *intended line.* That way, when you go to make your real stroke, you won't be lined up right or left of the hole.

A FIRMER GRIP

Many golfers have a death grip with all their clubs except the putter, which they hold like a delicate flower. My father felt it was important to have enough grip pressure on the putter to keep your putting stroke from getting wristy. He felt a good putting stroke was done with the arms and the shoulders, and not with the hands and the wrists.

DO WHAT WORKS

In some ways, John Houston, a very good and underrated tour player, is the most amazing putter I know. I don't think he putts as well as Brad Faxon or Ben Crenshaw, or Morris Hatalsky in his prime, but he's one of the best. And the amazing thing about his putting is that he takes no practice stroke. My father was a big believer in practice swings with every club; among other things, he said the practice swing or practice putting stroke is an effective way to eliminate tension. But for some people, the practice stroke *creates* tension. Or they waste their best swing in practice. My father never saw John on tour, but I know what he'd say about his unique approach to putting: If it works, keep doing it; putting is idiosyncratic.

THE 10 COMMANDMENTS OF PUTTING

Here are the *10 Commandments of Putting,* culled from my dad's notebooks:

I. Accelerate *through* the ball.
II. Keep the hands close together.
III. Putt with your eyes over the ball.
IV. Hit the top half of the ball to promote a smooth roll.
V. Play fast putts off the toe of the putter, but never play slow putts off the heel.
VI. Putt on the last hole just as you did on the first. (How often have you seen golfers give up in their putting during a bad round, as if putting didn't matter any more? The golfing gods remember that stuff; they'll get you next time.)
VII. (Mom's Rule) The putter should be soled level, not with the toe up.
VIII. On long putts, speed is more important than line.
IX. On short putts, line is critical. Get the line right, putt the ball on the line, give it enough hit, and the ball will go in.
X. (Robin's Rule) Follow through to the hole.

CHAPTER 12

An Open Door

I went to the 1996 U.S. Open—at Oakland Hills, on the outer rim of suburban Detroit, as Herbert Warren Wind used to say—with unusually powerful feelings. Early in the week, as I learned the nuances of the course and worked on my swing, I felt like I could predict everything that was going to happen over the course of the tournament. Getting in that state of preparedness is something I've been working on with Bob Rotella, my mental coach. I've been trying to see in my mind's eye every shot, from the opening tee shot on Thursday to the final putt on the 72nd hole on Sunday afternoon. Part of this mental preparation is to predict what your emotions are going to be, how excited or nervous you'll get, what your adrenaline will be doing, and how you'll respond to those different moods. (Rotella says that if you can go through the four rounds in your mind and not feel nervous you're not doing it right.) On Tuesday morning I could see myself holding up the trophy of the national champion, as my father used to call the U.S. Open winner. I could anticipate everything about the week, except how it would feel when it was all over. I wondered about my moment of triumph: Would I feel numb, would I feel joyful, would I become overwhelmed with thoughts about my father—those things I could not predict, they remained a mystery. I guess that's the ultimate goal of the athlete, to discover the *feeling* that accompanies a new achievement. I know sportscasters are mocked when they ask a triumphant athlete what they're feeling at that exact moment, but it's really the perfect question, even if the question is essentially unanswerable. Someday somebody is going to find a way to respond, and when they do the reply is going to be *extremely* interesting. Remember Michael Jordan after his team, the Chicago Bulls, won the 1996 NBA Championship? He hugged the ball as if it were a baby he had lost and recovered, and in his weeping you couldn't tell if he were happy or sad. I wondered what he was feeling, knowing all the while that some feelings don't lend themselves to words. I felt immense empathy for Michael at that moment. He lost his father prematurely, too.

When I got to the first tee on Thursday for the first round, I discovered that the breeze was blowing in a different direction than it had in the practice rounds. I had been hitting a 1-iron off the tee, but on Thursday, with the change in the wind, I said to Mark, "Driver?" He nodded in agreement. I was prepared for this kind of adjustment; during my practice rounds, I had thought about how practice rounds sometimes have nothing to do with what you encounter in an actual tournament.

I was nervous. I'm always nervous on the first tee of a tournament, and a little more nervous on the first tee of a major championship. There are only so many majors you can play in a career. Your play in majors is the way your career is ultimately going to be judged, by fans, by your peers, by writers, by yourself. Every weekly tour event is important, but the truth is if you screw up at Doral there's always Bay Hill down the road. Majors seem much more finite. If you're incredibly fortunate you might play in 70 or 80 when you're in your golfing prime. Through the end of 1996, I've played in 35, and I haven't won one yet. Standing on the first tee of Oakland Hills on Thursday, June 13, 1996, I thought—not consciously but deep down somewhere—that this would be the place where I'd win my first. I killed my drive, 300 yards, middle of the fairway.

Mark paced off the yardage to give me my distance to the hole.

"One-forty-seven," he said.

I double-checked it. I had the same.

"Just a little nine," I said. I wanted to bounce the ball to the hole.

Mark nodded, I grabbed the club, made a swing, caught it well—and watched the ball sail 20 yards over the green. For a split second, I felt sick. I knew immediately what had happened: We had paced off the distance from the wrong sprinkler head. I opened with a bogey when I should have started with a birdie or a par. In the end, in the U.S. Open I imagined myself winning, I finished a shot behind the winner. Did that wrong yardage keep me out of a playoff for the national championship? I would insist, *no.* Why? Because I was mentally prepared for a mental mishap. I would say it's almost impossible to go 72 holes without one. On the second hole of the tournament, I had a three-putt for par; you could say the same thing of a putt there, that that was the shot that kept me out of a playoff, that those two shots prevented me from winning the Open. The thing is, it doesn't work that way.

You win major championships, I've come to believe, not by playing a relentless series of great golf shots, but by being *prepared* for mishaps and setbacks. It's taken me a long time to realize this, but I think it's key, once you have enough golfing skill to win majors. Bob Rotella once asked Jack Nicklaus how often he played perfect golf in a major championship. "Oh, never," Nicklaus said. "I rarely played well at the majors. I won majors when I had no idea what I was doing, when I was just getting up and down from everywhere. You win majors by hanging around." Nicklaus was saying that to win majors, your thinking has to be better than your playing, and it's not realistic to expect either to be perfect. All it has to be is better than everybody else's.

I liked the golf course. Oakland Hills was playing long and wet, and those conditions certainly weighed in my favor. I knew right away that the course would reward patience and it would reward spectacular shots out of the rough, which was wet and exceedingly long and thick, or spectacular chips and putts. That, believe it or not, is not always the case; at Augusta, and at many British Opens, your best shots can turn out horrendously just because of the way the ball bounces. You have to take the bounces, good and bad, in stride. That's why a golfer with immense mental toughness, like Nicklaus, could play so well in the Masters and at the British Open year after year. Assessing my game when I arrived at Oakland Hills, there wasn't much to be impressed with; my ball-striking was shabby. But I didn't think that mattered very much.

My opening round was awful, in terms of hitting the golf ball. I made one birdie and hit about two fairways and about three greens, or so it seemed. But I grinded my way around and I was one over par after 18 holes, and that will never take you out of contention at a U.S. Open. In the second round, I played terrifically, yet shot only two strokes better than in the opening round: I made 17 pars, and my second birdie in 36 holes. In the third round, I made four bogeys and four birdies, without making a putt longer than 15 feet. That's level par for 54 holes. As Johnny Miller says, at an Open, pars wear white hats; they're the good guys. I was in contention because of my head, not because of my swing.

On Sunday, I was in the second-to-last group. Steve Jones and Tom Lehman were in the last group, right behind me. I was extremely nervous and I wasn't fighting it. How could I not be nervous? I was playing for the national championship. I made two birdies and a bogey going out and I was in better shape, in terms of the leaderboard, at the turn than before the day began. Asking for more from a front nine on a Sunday of a major is greedy. I made a bogey on 10 and a birdie on 11. On 12 I holed a 25-foot birdie putt, by far the longest putt I made all week. On 15 I had a 10-footer for a birdie. I knew if I could make that I'd be in very good shape to win the tournament. Before lining up that 10-footer, I took a long sip of water from a bottle Mark was carrying. By the time I was over the putt, there was not a drop of moisture in my throat. Nothing. I could not swallow. Rotella always says, "Find something, do *anything,* to take the pressure off. Say to yourself, 'It's just a pickup game.'" When I talk to Bob, it's over coffee in a nice restaurant somewhere, or over the phone while I'm lounging at home. Now I had to find a way to apply these civilized conversations to a moment of extreme intensity. I asked myself, "What do I do to make this putt?" When I'm at home I sometimes putt into Dru's feet. He shapes them like a "V" and I putt for the "V" and basically I never miss. So I turned the cup on the 15th green at Oakland Hills into Dru's feet. Meanwhile, Mark talked me into playing more break than I saw. The combination was effective: I made the putt on 15 and followed it with a par on 16.

Things were hairy now. Tom, Steve, and I were all in position to win the tournament—or to fold.

Standing on the 17th tee, knowing how the others stood, I figured that two pars would give me a very good chance at winning the Open and at worst would put me in a playoff. At a time like that, you want to know what you need to do in the overall sense before you get into the requirements of the shot you're about to play. Yes, you must play one shot at a time, but you'll play a different shot if you have to make a birdie. I wanted to know what I had to do to win the tournament. What I figured was that I needed to make two pars—on two of the most demanding closing holes in all of tournament golf, a long, uphill par-3 with an insanely difficult green, followed by a long, uphill par-4 with a similarly treacherous green. You can talk about 17 and 18 at Oakland Hills with the final two holes at Baltusrol and Oakmont and that's about it. I was as nervous as I have ever been in my life—and I was loving it.

The demands of the tee shot at 17 were formidable. The hole measures 200 yards, but uphill and into a slight breeze it was playing probably 220 yards. The green sits on the crown of a hill and slopes severely from back to front and from right to left. The front of the green is protected by six deep bunkers. Behind the green is a bunch of trees. Left of the green, down the hill, all there was was wet trampled grass mixed with mud, and with the flagstick on the left side of the green—forget about missing left. Right of the green was not much better. To make par, you had to knock it on the green. That's why they call it the U.S. Open.

I was between clubs. I knew if I smashed a 5-iron it would be too much. If I hit 6-iron and missed it at all I wouldn't reach the front of the green, and then I would be at the mercy of whatever lie the golfing gods gave me. So I hit the five. In making the swing, I held on just a little too long; in my effort to take a few yards off the shot, I never came fully through the swing. After the Open, people asked me if I heard a sudden sound that erupted in the middle of my backswing, from a hose suddenly shooting out water or air or something. The truthful answer is that I did hear it and it probably did distract me—and that's entirely my fault. Part of being mentally fit to win a major championship is to play through distractions. The distractions are there if you let them distract you. In talking about bad shots, I have one credo: *Never* make excuses.

The tee shot on 17 was bad. It went farther right and higher than I had planned, and it left me with a nasty downhill pitch to the hole. Even after playing the pitch shot well, I still had a 20-footer for par. I hit the par putt nearly as well as I could, but it ran out of steam and finished about a half-turn short of falling in. Somebody said, "The paint from the word *Titleist* should have been enough to make the putt drop." Well, it wasn't and it didn't. Bogey. I was disappointed, but not crushed. The national championship was still very much within my grasp.

On the 18th tee, I hit a 3-wood to make sure I stayed short of a bunker on the left side of the fairway about 300 yards off the tee. I hit the tee shot about 285 yards—when you're nervous your full shots will go farther than they normally do—just into the first cut of rough on the left side of the fairway. (Moments later, standing on the 18th tee, Tom Lehman hit a driver into the bunker to an awkward spot from which he couldn't get home. He closed with a bogey and also finished one shot back.) For my approach shot, I was again between a 5-iron and a six. I settled on the 6-iron and made a very good, strong, solid swing. The ball finished about 20 feet above the hole.

The putt I faced was extremely fast, *screaming* fast, and downhill. I knew the putt; it was one I had practiced, one I had seen before. Basically, it was a putt in which once you started the ball you could not keep it from going past the hole. I was trying to get the ball to the front edge of the hole, a place from which the ball could fall in. I was trying to give luck a chance. Even after I hit the putt, I thought I had hit it hard enough for it to trickle all the way to the hole. I was stunned to see the ball finish three feet short of the hole.

I knew what was riding on the three-footer. If I made it, and if Steve and Tom made pars on 18—and that was demanding a lot—there would be a three-way, 18-hole playoff for the title. I have never been more nervous in my life. I stood over the ball, and I could not get an image in my mind of me holing the putt. There was no way I was going to putt until I could get a picture of the putt dropping in my head. I backed off, swept away some flies that were swarming on the line of my putt. I got back over the ball. The putt was just like the first putt, except in miniature: downhill, very fast, right edge. I saw the ball falling in for par in my mind. I made a stroke. I thought it was a good one. I didn't watch the putt, just the spot where the ball was. I said to Mark later, "What did it do?" And he said, "It hit a lot of the hole. It just didn't drop." I had failed to hit the ball hard enough, and it went too far left.

Steve Jones made par to win. He had missed three years of golf because of a finger injury after an accident on a dirt bike. I was filled with awe for his comeback. My own disappointment was exceedingly deep. Had I stroked the putt before I was ready to, I would have been disappointed and *angry.* But I wasn't.

A lot of good players find blame in places other than themselves when they don't win. A bad bounce. Gallery noise. A spike mark. A sudden shift of wind. Anything. They think it's useful: "*Of course* the problem is not with me." I cannot do that, and it has everything to do with how I was raised. My life—my golfing life and the life I lead off the course too—is all about taking responsibility for my actions. I've gone over the 17th and 18th holes a thousand times in my mind, trying to come up with something to explain why I did not make pars. The only thing I can come up with is me. That's why I did not win that Open.

For all my good thinking before the tournament even began, my mind—and as a result my body—was unprepared for the feelings you experience when you need to two-putt from 20 downhill feet to get into a playoff for the U.S. Open. My body was not free enough to make the stroke I needed to make. I think I'll know next time. I really do.

During the back nine of the last round of the Open—the third Sunday in June, Father's Day—NBC aired a segment about my relationship with my father. (Tommy Roy, NBC's golf producer, called me several months before the Open to ask if I'd cooperate; he said he had a good feeling about me at Oakland Hills.) The piece was done very well and I know it was on a lot of people's minds as I was playing in. In the press tent after the round, a reporter asked me if my relationship with my father weighed on me, in either a positive or negative way, when I was trying to win the tournament. I said, "No," but I wasn't really answering the reporter's question. "No" meant that I didn't want to get into it. I didn't want my father and me to be the focus on a day when the heroic return of Steve Jones was the real story.

The truthful answer to the question is that there's still a little piece of me that has to come to terms with Dad's death, a little piece of me that has to prove to myself that I can win a U.S. Open, a Masters, a British Open, a PGA Championship—the tournaments I most want to win—without my father's physical presence. I let go of something that day with Butch Harmon on a practice tee in Japan in 1990. I let go of something more when I won The International five months later, and some more at the 1995 Masters and some more again at the 1996 U.S. Open. Nobody said it would be easy. Golf is a damn tough game, filled with heartache and with joy. So is life.

FAST GREENS

Growing up in the South, I didn't putt on greens that were especially fast. Most of the greens are Bermuda grass, which is thicker and slower than the Bent or Rye greens you find in most of the United States. The greens at a U.S. Open, which has never been played in the South, are generally somewhere between extremely fast and frighteningly fast. When I went to play in my first U.S. Open, I was nervous about the speed of the greens. My father gave me some advice that I've been using ever since. Fast greens, he reckoned, were easier to putt than slow greens because you could take a shorter stroke to move the ball the equivalent distance; the shorter the stroke, the better the chance to keep the stroke on the proper line. A 10-footer on a slow green is a 10-footer, but a 10-footer, by comparison, on a fast green is like a five-footer. A little stroke will get it to the hole. The same thing applies to downhill putts; downhill should be easier to get on line because it takes a shorter stroke than the big whack you have to give an uphill putt. Look, golf's hard; anything you can do to rationalize away a difficulty—like convincing yourself that U.S. Open greens are easier to putt than overwatered country-club greens—you should do.

OUT OF THE ROUGH

The first time I went to play in the Optimists Junior World at San Diego, I was unprepared for the rough. It was thick and snarly and it scared me. I was nervous and worried and upset. My father did not try to calm my nerves. His advice was mechanical: "Take the club outside and swing on a more upright plane than normal. That way the heel of the club, which is the part of the clubface that usually gets caught up in long grass, has less of a chance to snag." It wasn't poetic advice, but it was sound. Once I knew there was nothing really to be scared of, that there was a way to play out of deep rough, my nerves were settled. I wasn't afraid to hit driver. I didn't win the tournament, but I did learn how to hit a ball out of a tangled lie.

LEARN TO FORGET

A favorite phrase of my father's: "The inability to forget is devastating." Like a lot of the things he said, this had implications on and off the course. On the course, you have to be able to forget bad things or you will be doomed to repeat them. You're playing your home course, trying to break 80 for the first time. You need a par on the home hole for 79. The last time you were in this exact situation, you drove your tee shot out of bounds and finished with a snowman for eightysomething. Now, you're back on that same tee box again. You must forget what happened last time! If all you can do is think about it, that's devastating. It requires a lot of mental discipline to forget, but you have to learn to do it to become the golfer you're capable of being.

The best way I know to forget is to focus with extreme intensity on the present. What is the wind doing? Where is the flagstick today? Which way will the ball bounce on the fairway? What side of the tee box do I want to use? If the old dark thoughts can't be subverted, then you have no choice but to face them straight on. For instance, "OK—last time I went O.B. here because I was nervous, I swung too fast, my grip slipped because of perspiration. This time, I'm going to dry my hand with a towel before I start my swing, I'm going to take a deep breath before my backswing to slow me down, I'm going to lighten my grip pressure, and I'm going to aim left and swing straight to my target."

IN THE WIND

My father was something of an expert on golf in the wind, probably because of all the golf he played in Texas. Maybe that's why he liked golf in the British Isles, and the British Open in particular, so much. He said that when playing a shot into the wind, don't swing too hard. "When it's breezy, hit it easy," was how he put it. The reason is that the easier you hit the ball, the less spin you impart to it and the lower the ball will go.

ONE SHOT AT A TIME

Sometimes when my father and I were playing a new course, I'd tell him how to play a hole, where to drive it, where to play the approach shot, what side of the flagstick to be on. I'd be lining up my eagle putt on the tee. And then I'd hear my father say, "Don't get ahead of yourself." He believed that good golfers didn't play holes, they played individual shots. Play each shot well, you've played the hole well. Play all the holes well, you've played the round well. Golf's most common cliche is also one of its truest statements: Play one shot at a time. I know the TV interviewers go crazy when they hear a golfer in contention talking about his game plan and saying those words, but they are the ultimate golf mantra of the expert player.

REPAID IN FULL

To achieve a degree of excellence in golf—in anything, I'm sure—you make sacrifices. As a teenager, there were a lot of days when my friends were going to the beach, hanging out and goofing off, while I was on the lesson tee, learning to control the height of my wedge shots. There were many nights in high school and college when I would leave parties at 10 P.M., just when the parties were starting to get good, so that I could be well-rested for a 7:30

tee time the following morning. I often thought, "Other people are having more fun than I am." I didn't resent them because of it; I had chosen the life I was leading, but I knew there were things I was missing out on.

But now, and I don't mean to brag when I say this, I think I'm having more fun than most people. When I'm in an airport or at a gas station or at a golf tournament, and somebody I don't know wants to talk about golf, I can understand why. A lot of people spend their working lives saving up enough money so that in retirement they can do what we do, which is play golf every day—except on days when we're fishing or hunting. A lot of people wish they could someday, just once, shoot the kind of score we can shoot on our worst day. Being a touring pro is not just a marvelous way to make a living, it's a wonderful way of life. I play the game I love for my job. I stay in nice hotels. I eat in good restaurants. I have good friends on the tour. I try never to forget how good I have it, although I know at times I have. And since the stranger in the airport or at the gas station makes my good fortune possible, I feel it's incumbent upon me to answer his questions, to talk to him about his upcoming trip to Scotland, to ask him about the soft-spike policy at his home course. After all, we're both golfers, so we do speak a common language. (I am, however, going to have to print up business cards to hand out to young single waitresses, reading: "No, I *cannot* introduce you to Tiger Woods.")

RESTORING RHYTHM

I have never known a golfer whose rhythm didn't get fouled up from time to time. Even the sweetest of the sweet-swingers—Fred Couples, Fuzzy Zoeller, Steve Elkington—they all get swinging too fast every so often. My father had a wonderful drill for restoring rhythm: He had me hit balls with my left hand only. In the swing, nothing can go faster than the left arm, and it is the left arm more than any other single thing that controls the swing. By swinging with just your left arm you *can't* swing that fast. After you do that for a while, put your right hand back on with the thought that it's just there for the ride. It's not there to rev things up.

TIGER WOODS

The man of the moment, in golf, as he probably will be for the next 20 to 40 years, is Tiger Woods. His popularity, particularly among people who do not know a divot from a ball mark, is astonishing, and absolutely wonderful for golf. Within golf circles, I find it very heartening that Woods is being cheered on by all segments of the golfing population, whites and blacks, Asians and Hispanics, private-club golfers and public-course players, men and women, the young, the middle-aged, the elderly. When you see so many different groups of people responding to Woods so positively, it fills you with hope that we may be entering an age where people are seeing people for what they are, and not for what they look like.

I was flattered that when Woods turned pro he sought me out to show him around a little bit, not that he needed much showing around. We played a few practice rounds together. He'd ask questions about particular courses and tournaments. Our approach to the game is similar, and his teacher, Butch Harmon, has taught me extensively. We both play Titleist clubs and balls. We're both serious about our play.

One thing I noticed about Tiger right away is how well he chooses his club for tee shots on par-4s. That takes real maturity to do properly. It took me probably five years on tour before I really knew when to hit a regular driver, when to rip a driver, when to hit 1-iron, when to hit 3-wood. When you're a long hitter, those decisions become critical because there are generally more hazards in play for long hitters, but there's also more opportunity for reward for the well-played tee shot.

In fact, in our one-hole playoff at the Las Vegas Invitational, Tiger out-thought me on the tee shot. We had drawn slips of paper for the honor; I hit driver and I nailed it, 310 yards, right in the middle of the fairway. Tiger, hugely experienced in match play, did *not* take out a driver and try to fly one by mine, which a less experienced golfer with his length might have done. But neither did he hit the conservative 2-iron, which is what he had been hitting off the 18th tee during the tournament. He chose a 3-wood and he hit it straight and true. His ball finished just a few yards behind my own. Perfect for Tiger, for now he had the chance to play first. He hit a 9-iron to about 18 feet, well within birdie range. First on is always an advantage in match play. I hit a dumb shot, got a little handsy with an 8-iron, and pulled the shot into the back left bunker. My bunker shot left me with six feet for par. Woods took two putts for par. My stroke on my par putt was good, but my read was not; the ball stayed out and Tiger had his first victory.

I was genuinely happy for Tiger and very pleased for golf, much as I was when Ben Crenshaw beat me by a shot to win the 1995 Masters. Tiger is supremely confident, without being arrogant or obnoxious. He's smart, friendly, curious, serious. He is consumed with winning and with improvement. He is definitely not playing golf just for money. His will is off the charts. I don't think he has the flair for putting that Seve Ballesteros had at his prime, but he's like Seve in that he can *will* putts in when he needs them. I think he will spur the other leading golfers in the game to improvement. I don't know a greater compliment to pay him.

TARGET GOLF

When my father and Bob Toski wrote *How to Feel a Real Golf Swing,* they asked Bob Rotella, the sports psychologist, to write an afterword. I was pleased by that, because before that I didn't know how open my father was to the contributions psychologists can make to the game. Subsequently, I began to work closely with Bob, as do Tom Kite, Brad Faxon, Nick Price, Billy Mayfair, and Pat Bradley, among many others.

The thrust of Bob's message can be summarized in a sentence: "Get into the process, not the result." The process is taking your stance, getting a good waggle, staring down the "C" in a sign that says "CBS Sports," if that's your target on a particular shot. Bob encourages his players to become very target-oriented. Often the target is the hole itself. If a player responds to an aggressive thought, Bob will say, "Knock down that flagstick!" Sometimes the target is a limb of a tree with a gentle draw; if you get that part down, everything else will take care of itself.

Bob loves the way Greg Norman and Corey Pavin stare down their target line hard before they make a swing. They practically burn it down with their stares. As I think about this, I realize it's not surprising that my father responded so strongly to Bob. Dr. Rotella is saying, with different language, the same thing my father's mentor, Harvey Penick, said: *Take dead aim.*

CHAPTER 13

The Next Generation

I hope my children become golfers. I don't care whether they become professional golfers or not, but I'd be sad if they didn't enjoy the game for the game's sake. When I'm an old man, I want to play golf with them, and with their children. I'd love to see my children play golf with my mother. With the possible exception of religion, I don't know any single thing that can teach a value system to a young person the way golf can. And golf is a lot more fun than Sunday school.

You want to teach children to play by the rules, you teach them golf. You want to teach children to respect the rights of others, you teach them golf. You want to teach children to tell the truth, to be responsible for their own actions, to control their emotions, you teach them golf. You want children to learn to appreciate the outdoors and the beauty of a piece of land and the drama of a sunset, you teach them golf. And while they're learning, they're having the time of their lives.

You can't go wrong with golf. People make friends through golf. They travel to beautiful places through golf. Sometimes golfing children grow up to find a way to make a living in the game, as I have been lucky enough to do, as my father was lucky enough to do. There are more golf-related jobs now than ever before. But that should never be the motivation. The important thing is to introduce young people to the game, to see if the seed will take root.

Whether it will or not, there's no way to tell in advance. I have often wondered what sort of personality type is attracted to the game, and I've come up with . . . nothing. For one thing, there are degrees of dedication; some people really get bitten by the golf bug, while others like the game, but it's not a driving force in their lives. Some people can enjoy golf visiting it only periodically. There are casual people, neurotic people, athletic people, unathletic people—all attracted to the game in differing degrees. On tour, the most commonly found personality type is the perfectionist, although I don't notice that as a typical trait among ordinary avid amateur golfers. What is undeniably true is that if you're not introduced to the game, if you don't have any way of finding your way to the game, then you can't become a golfer. The role of the parent, I believe, is to introduce the child to the sport, then to watch from behind a tree. Pushing golf always backfires; the child may become a golfer, but not a happy one.

When Lexie and Dru were very young, I'd bring them with me when I went to practice my putting. They could run around on the greens, see how many balls they could get into a single golf cup, toss back balls to me, fiddle with the clubs in my bag. They got a sense for what the game is about without my ever having to say a word. Late in the winter of 1996, Dru has just turned three and Lexie is eight. Dru seems to be already taking to the game. He's interested in hitting *anything:* golf balls, baseballs, occasionally his sister. Lexie is more interested in other things: horses, computers, piano. Someday, maybe, she'll take more of an interest in golf. She's very close to my mother and she sees how much fun my mother has playing golf. On the other hand, she also sees how golf requires me to be away from home half the nights in a year, the only bad part about my job. If she has mixed feelings about the game, it's totally understandable. The only thing I plan to do is to encourage her if she tells me she wants to play.

I don't think I'm going to be able to teach my children the game the way my father taught me. For one thing, my father was a professional teacher; he knew what he was doing. I'm a lousy teacher. Every time I try to tell my mother something about the swing I usually wind up confusing her and making things worse. With Robin, I'm even worse, but I'd like to think the problem is as much her as it is me. This is a woman—married to a professional golfer—who thinks nothing of using a "hand wedge" to get herself out of a greenside bunker. Unlike me, Mark is a wonderful teacher for Mom, and he'd probably be a wonderful teacher for Lexie and Dru, if he had the time and inclination. But his life is just as busy. On November 20, 1996, he and his wife, Lynn, had their first baby, Lowrey. Between his caddying work, our golf-course design business, his own golf, and his growing family, it will be hard for him to find the time to teach as well. But I can't imagine a better teacher for my kids. He's patient, generous with his time, kind, tolerant of mistakes. He's a natural teacher.

Mark and I were always trying to get Dad to watch us hit balls and give us lessons, but in general the parent is probably not the best golf instructor for a child. When I make the mistake of trying to tell Lexie something about her swing it's usually a disaster. Brad Faxon was visiting with us once and he saw Lexie struggling to hit a ball, and he said, "Put your thumbs down the shaft, not around it," and he gave her a demonstration. "Good. Now when you make your swing, don't let your hands move." And right away she just started killing it. So I said, "Shoot, when I try to tell her something, she just runs off crying." "Of course," said Brad. "You're her father." It's not every parent who can teach their children the game. That's why there are professional teachers.

I remember once when Mark and I were young, we were on the practice tee with my father and there was another father out there with his two sons. And that father was giving his sons a lot of "Do this" and "Don't do that." The kids were red-faced and frustrated and ready to burst. My father shook his head. "Maybe they'll become good golfers," he said, "but I doubt they'll ever enjoy the game." No matter how playful you are with your children when teaching them golf, there may be something in the chemistry that makes you not the right teacher for them. I was lucky. Your kids might be better off with your friendly neighborhood PGA professional.

Still, I couldn't see Lexie and Dru taking any kind of formal instruction until they're at least 12 years old or so. Kids have a natural instinct for the game that most adults do not. You tell them to go hit a ball and they will pretty much show you flawless form. I don't think you develop bad habits by playing golf as a kid without training; I think that's how a child finds and develops his natural swing. Later, the professional teacher can work on shaping that natural swing.

I hope that Lexie and Dru will find things in their lives that will motivate them the way golf did for me. I'm starting to see that with Lexie and horses. She loves everything about horses. If she has a science project for school, she wants to do something related to horses. Now she's at the point where if she wants to go riding, or have a riding lesson, or go to a horse show, then she has to do her homework, be nice to her mom and dad, mind her manners, help out around the house. Her interest in horses has become a powerful motivator. Maybe horses will be a lifelong interest for her. But she's also being introduced to piano and dance and gymnastics and soccer and painting and reading. Their world is so rich in interesting things to do, and I would never want my kids to think it begins and ends with golf. But I'm prejudiced in favor of the game. Golf is civilized, and the world today often is not. Golf *is* a game for a lifetime.

If golf continued as a family business for us, I'd be pleased. In 1994, Mark and I started a golf-course design company. We have two employees: Paul Cowley, who has an extensive background in landscape design, and Bob Spence, who knows golf as a touring pro, club pro, club manager, and course designer and builder. My friend David Blackshear also works for the company, in a more informal way, keeping his eyes and ears open for projects for which we might be a good fit, and following up on calls we get about potential projects. Through the end of 1996, we have two courses up and running. One is a daily-fee course in Kingsland, Georgia, called Laurel Island Links. The other is a resort course on Fripp Island, South Carolina, called Ocean Creek. The Fripp Island course is a beauty, with great views of marshes and dunes and ocean, and there are very few houses. They filmed parts of *Forrest Gump* right on the golf course, and the movie *Jungle Book,* too. The Kingsland course is a par 72, 7,100 yards from the backs, with a lot of marsh, while many of the holes wind their way through Georgia pines and giant live oaks. We have two courses under construction. If someday that might be a business that Dru and Lexie were interested in, that would be wonderful.

My taste in golf course architecture is very traditional. I love Cypress Point, Augusta National, Pine Valley, the No. 2 course at Pinehurst. I was very fortunate to get a private tutorial from an architect, Rees Jones, who I think works in the tradition of Alister Mackenzie and A.W. Tillinghast and Donald Ross. Rees is the son of an architect, Robert Trent Jones, and the brother of an architect, Robert Trent Jones, Jr., but he is very much his own man. He designed the new course at Sea Island, Ocean Forest, where Mark and my mom and I are members and where the 2001 Walker Cup will be played. My friend Bill Jones III, the chairman of the Sea

Island Co. and the force behind Ocean Forest, was kind enough to ask Rees if I could tag along as Rees laid out and oversaw the construction of Ocean Forest. Rees was happy for me to do so. He liked the idea of having a tour player, a club member, a Sea Island Co. board member, and a friend of Bill's alongside him. But I feel I had the better end of the deal: I learned from a master. I like the idea of working with other people. I don't get to do that much in my day job.

My first goal as an architect is to change popular opinion about what a modern course is. Modern courses can be built in the traditional manner, with deep bunkers and wide fairways and short distances between greens and tees, where the first concern is for walkers, not for riders. Sometimes developers, the people with money behind the construction of a golf course, need a golfing education. They've been to the great money-making resorts, but not to the little gems. In the 1980s and 1990s, it seemed that developers wanted to spend the most money they possibly could to build golf courses that would be just dazzling, stupendous. The education comes in saying, "Stupendous is not the goal. *Pleasing* is the goal." Cypress, Augusta, Pinehurst No. 2—they *fascinate* you. There's nothing freakish about them. The courses we want to build, and that we have built, cost a lot less than most courses being built today. Some people are calling this approach to golf-course architecture the "minimalist school." It certainly didn't start with me; architects like Tom Doak and Ben Crenshaw and Donald Steel have been talking about these principles all their designing lives. But I feel very confident that the philosophy of less is more is critical to the future of golf-course design, for reasons of ecology, economy and aesthetics. Less is more is the future because it has had such a good past. There has never been a period for American golf courses like the 1920s and 1930s. I'd like to return to the simple notions that made so many of those courses so memorable.

One of the most pleasing projects I've worked on so far is a tiny golf course I built for Bill Jones and his family in their ancestral hunting grounds south of Sea Island, a large tract called Cabin Bluff. Bill wanted a small, manageable course near the hunting cabins that would still constitute real golf, and he asked me to design it and for my company to construct it. Paul Cowley and I came up with a three-hole course on which each hole has three sets of tees and three holes on each of the three greens (they're large). In other words, you can play an 18-hole, par 72, 6,800-yard course that occupies only 30 acres. I could imagine the day coming when the small-scale private course is far more common than it is today, the ultimate backyard toy for those who can afford it.

My father was very interested in course design. Sometimes after dinner we'd draw holes on graph paper, where each little block would represent 10 yards. Sometimes we did it on drafting paper. He did a lot of consulting in the days when they didn't call it consulting. People would ask him about moving tees or expanding greens or narrowing fairways; they wanted to know what he thought. He was friends with Pete Dye, the golf-course architect, and he learned a lot from Pete about course design. He and friends talked periodically about trying to build and run a golf course, but in the end he always decided that the thing he loved most and did best was teach. Part of his decision, I think, not to become a golf entrepreneur was that he knew it would diminish the amount of time he could spend with Mark and me. He is the model I hold up for myself. As I get older, my goal is to make time for my children the way my father did for me.

I love playing tournament golf, but I don't like being away from Robin and the children. They travel with me as much as possible, but as the kids get older that becomes harder to do. In recent years, I've started flying on a private jet right in and out of Sea Island. I lease a certain number of hours per year. It's very expensive, but it gives me probably an extra 20 nights at home over the course of a year because it's so much more efficient than flying on commercial airlines. There's no question to me that it's money well spent. The planes I fly in always have two pilots, and the pilots know that my preference is to endure any amount of inconvenience if it means not flying in really bad weather. I'm friends with a lot of the pilots and have learned a lot about flying. When I was flying home with my mom and Robin and Mark and the kids from the 1996 U.S. Open, the pilots were asking about what kind of jet I'd be interested in leasing in the future. I said, "I was a three-putt away from *buying* a *big* jet." They thought that was funny. Maybe someday I'll become a pilot myself. It would be another way for me to address my father's death.

There are still so many things I want to do as a golfer. I'm 32 now. I'm going to do everything I can do to make these next 10 years as productive as they can possibly be. The Ryder Cup is a major motivator for me; I want to play on every Ryder Cup team between now and when I'm 50. I'd love to play for Tom Kite when he captains the team in 1997. Someday, I expect, Curtis Strange and Ben Crenshaw and Paul Azinger will all be Ryder Cup captains, and I'd love to play for them. I dream of someday being a Ryder Cup captain myself.

The greatest joy of representing the United States on the 1996 Presidents Cup team was the chance to spend a week with Arnold Palmer, who was the team's captain. Growing up, I was a Jack Nicklaus fan, but my father was mesmerized by Arnold—not because of the way he swung, but because of the way he played. At one of the dinners during the Presidents Cup, for just the players and their guests, Arnold was talking to us about our responsibility to the game. He said it was our responsibility to make sure the young players coming up now learned from us just as we learned from the veterans when we were joining the tour. He said it was critical to respect the traditions of the game. He said our biggest responsibility was to those who love the game; we needed to be generous with our time and energy to the game's true fans. "My father instilled that in me, and I want to instill that in you," Arnold said. Then he nodded in my direction. "Davis knows what I'm talking about. He grew up in the game just like I did. He had the kind of relationship with his father that I had with mine."

Robin couldn't even look at me. I don't know if I ever felt more proud to be the son of Davis Love, Jr., than I was at that moment. I knew then that anything I had ever sacrificed to achieve something in golf was a sacrifice well made. Arnold's comments reminded me that I owe the game a lot more than it owes me, and that every time I play, and on every shot I take, I'm playing for myself, for my family—and for my father.

Someday, far, far off in the future, I hope, I'll come to the realization that I can't beat Tiger Woods anymore. I'll have won, I hope, this tournament and that tournament, and I'll show up for this dinner and that practice round, and I'll enjoy being one of golf's old men, telling stories, watching the new talent come up, traveling the world with Robin, building golf courses, hunting, fishing, hanging out with my kids and, I hope, their kids. That would be the life.

In a day or two, I'll leave St. Simons and head out to California to begin a new year of golf, the 1997 season, my 12th on tour. If my father were alive today, he'd have already reviewed with me his notes for the new year. He'd have thumbed through his legal pads and made the lists of things I'd need to do to play better golf in 1997 than I did in 1996. I'd like to think at this point I'm pretty much taking stock of the inventory the way he would have done it himself. Dad would probably have two new files by this point, one for Lexie's golf, another for Dru's. He'd be 61 now. He never talked about becoming a grand old man of golf. I don't think he ever imagined himself retired from teaching. He never met his namesake, Davis M. Love IV. He would have loved Dru, Dru's spirit, his buoyancy, his alertness. I thank God he was able to know Lexie, however briefly. I remember Dad cradling her, shortly before the accident, when Lexie was not even six months old. My father never had a sister, he never had a daughter, and now he had this tiny beautiful sleeping girl in his arms. He rocked her gently back and forth. He gave her rhythm before she could walk. And then he was gone.